The Thinking Student's Guide to College

CHICAGO GUIDES TO ACADEMIC LIFE

....

The Thinking Student's Guide to College

75

Tips for Getting a Better Education

Andrew Roberts

THE UNIVERSITY OF
CHICAGO PRESS
....
CHICAGO AND LONDON

Andrew Roberts is assistant professor of political science at Northwestern University and fellow at the Institute for Policy Research. He is the author of *The Quality of Democracy in Eastern Europe: Public Preferences and Policy Reforms*. His research focuses on the politics of Eastern Europe, democratization, and public policy.

The University of Chicago Press, Chicago 60637
The University of Chicago Press, Ltd., London
© 2010 by The University of Chicago
All rights reserved. Published 2010
Printed in the United States of America

19 18 17 16 15 14 13 12 11 10   1 2 3 4 5

ISBN-13: 978-0-226-72114-9 (cloth)
ISBN-13: 978-0-226-72115-6 (paper)
ISBN-10: 0-226-72114-0 (cloth)
ISBN-10: 0-226-72115-9 (paper)

Library of Congress Cataloging-in-Publication Data

Roberts, Andrew Lawrence, 1970–
    The thinking student's guide to college : 75 tips for getting a better education / Andrew Roberts.
        p. cm. — (Chicago guides to academic life)
    ISBN-13: 978-0-226-72114-9 (cloth: alk. paper)
    ISBN-10: 0-226-72114-0 (cloth: alk. paper)
    ISBN-13: 978-0-226-72115-6 (pbk.: alk. paper)
    ISBN-10: 0-226-72115-9 (pbk.: alk. paper)
    1. College choice—United States. 2. Education, Higher—Aims and objectives. 3. Universities and colleges—United States. 4. College student orientation. 5. College students—Conduct of life. I. Title. II. Series: Chicago guides to academic life.
    LB2350.5.R634 2010
    378.1'98—dc22

                                                            2009049905

CONTENTS

Introduction

What do you want out of college? If it is just a diploma and a good time, this is not the book for you. Nor will I provide much advice on getting along with your roommate or balancing your studies and your social life. Even if what you want is straight As, you should probably look elsewhere. There are already dozens of books that will help you in these areas.

If, on the other hand, you think that college should be a place where professors challenge you to do the best you are capable of, provide you with personalized feedback on your work, and show you new ways of understanding the world, then you are in the right place. This book will show you how to get such an education.

You might assume that such advice is not necessary, that all colleges are designed to lead you by the hand and draw out the best that is in you (the word "educate" comes from the Latin *e + ducere*, or "draw out"). After all, that is their reason for being. As a card-carrying member of the academic guild, I won't tell you that this is wrong. They might take away my card. What I will say is that colleges and universities do many things, only some of which are geared to giving undergraduates the best possible education.

Universities, for example, must please their alumni and donors for whom a first-class football team may be more important than a better learning experience. They also take it as their mission to train the next generation of professors—that means graduate students, not you. Most are committed to creating new knowledge, an activity known as research, which is not necessarily a boon to teaching. Universities even have to make sure that we faculty are happy and won't run off to the business world where salaries are better. As the University of California's Clark Kerr memorably put it, the job of the college president is to provide "parking for the faculty, sex for the students, and athletics for the alumni."

Some of these activities (I haven't listed all of them here) may contribute to your education or simply make it possible at a (somewhat) reasonable price.[1] Others, however, may get in your way. Universities gather too many smart people in one place to completely prevent you from getting a great undergraduate education. Unfortunately, most universities also have a path of least resistance where less ambitious and uninformed students float by, getting far less out of college than they could.

This book is not addressed to less ambitious students. It is addressed to the uninformed who want more, but do not know how to get it. It is for those students who want to be challenged, who want to produce original and consequential work, who want to be exposed to new ways of thinking, who want in short to leave college a different and better person than they entered it.

I was inspired to write this book by students who, after four years of higher learning, realized that they should have been doing something different. That in place of rote learning and impersonal interactions, they should have taken classes from engaged professors who challenged them to think creatively and produce meaningful work.

I have met many such students. Often they come to me during their senior year seeking a letter of recommendation and I can barely recall them from the giant lecture class they took with me. I ask them if they might not ask another professor who knows them better, but they claim that I am the one they feel closest to. Sometimes I ask them about the accomplishment in their college career they are proudest of and they have trouble recalling one.

These students are inevitably smart and hardworking, and I am continually amazed that they have completed college without finding a subject they genuinely cared about, writing a paper they truly believed in, or meeting a professor who gave them more than the time of day. This book is an attempt to avert these lost opportunities and give more students the chance to get the best possible education they can. Its aim is to turn sighs of "I wish I had known" and "I wish I had done things differently" into shouts of "I wouldn't have done it any other way."

---

1. In fact, universities set their prices below costs in order to attract more students than they can admit and increase their cachet by being choosy among them. See Gordon C. Winston, "The Economic Structure of Higher Education: Subsidies, Consumer Inputs, and Hierarchy," Williams College Project on the Economics of Higher Education, DP-4, 1996.

The book does this in a specific way. It does not teach study skills, how to get As, or how to navigate the social scene. For those interested in getting a better education, such advice is hardly necessary, and as I mentioned above dozens of books already cover these topics. I am also not going to take you on a tour of actual colleges. There are plenty of books that do that already and emphasize trivial or nonexistent differences while ignoring enormous similarities.

What this book does is give you an insider's look at how universities deliver an education. Its view is from the ground floor, from what I believe is the fundamental interaction in a university education: the relationship between students and professors. While this might seem like the element of university life that is easiest to navigate, it is in fact the place where you will face some of the highest barriers to getting the best education you can.

Consider the following contrast. Joe Ordinary goes to the top-ranked school that he gets into, chooses its two most popular majors, and takes their highest-rated courses, most of them large lecture classes. He also graduates without meeting any of his professors, without producing any work that he is proud to call his own, without having explored any fields he didn't know beforehand, and with a mountain of student loans.

Jane Extraordinary, by contrast, chooses a less selective (and cheaper) school but opts for a smaller, offbeat major where she gets a lot of individualized attention, makes friends with several of her professors, and ends up coauthoring a paper with one of them. Because she leaves school without much debt, she spends her first year after graduation doing charitable work in a foreign country and returns home to attend a PhD program (OK, this last part is wishful thinking on my part).

While I would not shed tears over the fate of Joe, I would argue that he has not gotten as much out of college as he could have. And I think he may agree with me. He has surely become credentialed and will succeed in a job market that rates those credentials highly. But he has also spent over $200,000 for an education that he probably could have gotten for a fraction of the cost. He has not taken advantage of even a fraction of the resources that a university has to offer. Jane did this and has gotten a better education not to mention more value for her tuition dollar.

A recent survey confirms that these differences are large and widespread. It asked students at over a thousand colleges and universities how much their university challenged them academically and gave them an enriching educational experience among other things.[2] The results were striking. At every college, there was a lot of variation. Some students felt they were constantly being challenged to do better and had lots of interaction with professors and an enriching education experience, while others felt just the opposite. What varied was not the universities—the same pattern showed up everywhere, from Harvard to Podunk U—but the students. Some students managed to suck the juice out of their college, while others were left with the rind. The aim of this book is to show you how to find the juice.

Just to make clear what I am aiming for, I view a great education as maximizing the amount of personal interaction between committed students and great professors. In an anecdote I will return to, my ideal is a smart and caring professor on one end of a log and a student (or handful of students) on the other. It envisions students solving complex problems under the guidance of an experienced mentor and receiving constant feedback on their efforts. It exposes students to as many new ideas and styles of thinking as possible. It tries to identify and sharpen students' natural talents, while not neglecting their weaknesses.

As you might guess, few American universities offer exactly such an education. At least three obstacles stand in the way. The first is cost: it would be prohibitively expensive to give all students the personal attention they want from truly qualified faculty members. The second is research: universities today are structured around producing knowledge rather than teaching students for reasons I explain in chapter 1. The third is incentives: professors have few incentives to devote themselves to giving students the best possible education and many incentives to teach undergraduates in a perfunctory way.[3]

While these obstacles make it harder to have a great learning experience, they do not make it impossible. You simply need to learn how to do it. The trick is to know how universities work. All universities have what I will call, for lack of a better term, loopholes, which give you access to the sort of personalized education I have just described. They are hidden in such institutions as mandatory office hours, drop-add periods, research assistantships,

2. See the National Survey of Student Engagement, *Promoting Engagement for All Students: The Imperative to Look Within: 2008 Results*, Indiana University Center for Postsecondary Research, www.nsse.iub.edu. It is discussed at more length in chapter 2.

3. A fourth obstacle is that many students, hopefully not those reading this book, do not wish to be challenged and work hard; they view college as a time to relax and socialize.

honors programs, and senior theses. Universities make ends meet because most students do not take advantage of these loopholes. What I will show you is how to exploit the system as it is currently set up so that you do get personalized attention from committed professors.

In the process, I will also try to demystify the workings of universities. Most students spend four years at college without understanding what makes the place tick. Few have any idea what professors do in the hours when they are not teaching and what sort of relationship they have with teaching. They have a vague idea that something called research goes on at the university, but don't know what it means or how it affects them for good or ill. My hope is that by explaining how universities work, I will make it easier for students to get the most out of them.

Some of the questions I will explore are the following. What makes some universities different from others and all of them similar to each other? What motivates professors, and why are some better teachers than others? How do you identify the best professors and get them to devote attention to you? What should you look for in choosing a college, courses, and a major? And how can you improve your education outside the classroom?

The book itself is structured around a list of tips for getting a better education. I have done this to make reading easier. Indeed, readers may skip around among the tips as they please with little loss of comprehension. None of the tips are hard and fast and a few contradict each other, at least in part. (There is more than one way to skin a cat.) I had originally called them rules, but that word is too strong. I will not hesitate to qualify the tips in the text that follows them, but I will often state them a little more bluntly than is necessary to get my point across. While many students deduce the tips I set out by themselves, many do not or lose too much time before they do.

What are my qualifications for offering this guidance? I am not an expert on education (I am in fact a political scientist), though I have tried to immerse myself in the latest research on pedagogy (or the science of learning). I have spent a good deal of time working in higher education and thinking about where students stumble and where they succeed. My main qualification I think is that I made a good number of mistakes in my college career. I regret not taking advantage of more opportunities at college, and this book is partially a biography of my errors as well as those of students I have taught. I hope readers of this book will learn and profit from my mistakes.

THE PURPOSES OF A COLLEGE EDUCATION

What should you get out of college? In this text box, the first of many scattered throughout the book, I'd like to describe one scholar's attempt to articulate the aims of a university education. Derek Bok, whose arguments I paraphrase below, is a former president of Harvard and has written widely about higher education. He believes that students should aim for eight things during their university stay. Unfortunately, he thinks that universities fall short in these areas; therefore it is incumbent upon you to find ways to achieve these goals.*

1. Learning to communicate. This means learning both how to write and how to communicate orally. These are skills that virtually all employers want, but ones where American students frequently come up short. To gain these skills you need to seek out courses that force you to write and speak and at the same time deliver constant feedback on your progress (see Tip 14).

2. Learning to think. This means learning how to think critically (see Tip 50). The goal is to be able to attack complicated problems without certain solutions, an activity that characterizes just about every job students will ultimately find themselves doing. Acquiring this skill requires you to seek out courses where professors challenge you to work your way through exactly such problems. It also requires sequentially building on your knowledge so that each course extends your abilities.

3. Building character. Though universities no longer try to inculcate moral values as they once did, you should seek out classes that will help you to deal with the ethical dilemmas that you will face in your life. These classes won't tell you what to do, but they will show you how to reason through these problems to identify the core issues at play and introduce you to a variety of ethical theories that can guide your decisions. Participating in community service activities also serves this end.

4. Preparing for citizenship. American democracy is plagued by citizens who care little about politics and know even less. College is one place where you can increase your interest in and knowledge of politics. You can do this both in coursework—Bok recommends classes in Ameri-

* The book where they appear is entitled *Our Underachieving Colleges: A Candid Look at How Much Students Learn and Why They Should Be Learning More* (Princeton, NJ: Princeton University Press, 2006).

can government, political philosophy, economics, and American foreign policy—as well as by participating in student government or other civic-minded organizations like the College Democrats or Republicans.

5. *Living with diversity.* Unlike many countries, America is a multi-cultural society, and one of the things that you can learn at college is an appreciation of the different cultures that make up our country, whether African American, Latino, or Muslim to name just a few. Good universities sponsor workshops and lectures to acquaint students with this diversity, and it is worthwhile to attend these functions with an open mind and to make efforts to get to know students of other cultures in extracurricular activities (see Tip 67).

6. *Preparing for a global society.* As the world becomes more globalized, it behooves students to learn more about the world outside America, in order both to succeed in the global economy and to become better citizens. You can pursue this knowledge in a number of places like coursework devoted to understanding a particular foreign culture, language classes (see Tip 31), study abroad programs (see Tip 23), and even interacting with foreign students (see Tip 68).

7. *Acquiring broader interests.* Colleges have long tried to expose students to the great achievements of human civilization whether in art, literature, philosophy, or science. Studying these works not only improves your thinking skills, it also provides you with the cultural foundation to interact with other intelligent people. Universities have a variety of ways of doing this (see Tip 8), though if you truly want to develop broad interests, you will likely need to go beyond these requirements.

8. *Preparing for a career.* Many students look to college to provide them with vocational skills. While not all universities are designed to do this, you can benefit from classes in vocational majors like business, engineering, and education. At the same time, you should not neglect the liberal arts, not only because of the more general skills they provide but also because so many students change their initial career choice as they wend their way through the workforce.

1 How Universities Work

··

Soon after arriving on campus, freshmen at my undergraduate college were treated to a lecture by an art historian entitled "A Sense of Where You Are." His talk was about the architectural evolution of the campus and the merits of its various buildings. This chapter tries to do something similar but at a more general level. It explains how modern universities and colleges work— not their physical architecture, but their internal architecture. What they are trying to do—their mission—and how they carry it out.[1] The point of this exercise is to show you what sort of education universities have been designed to provide. The advice throughout this book will make better sense if you understand why I am offering it.

There are over four thousand colleges and universities in the United States, ranging from for-profit, vocational schools that teach their classes online to nonprofit, liberal arts colleges in small New England villages. The description and advice to follow applies to a fraction, but a significant fraction of this group: colleges and universities that try to maintain a national reputation and have faculty who produce at least some research, though many of the factors described apply more broadly.[2] Lest one think this is

---

1. Much of the analysis here is based on Gordon C. Winston, "The Decline in Undergraduate Teaching: Moral Failure or Market Pressures," Williams Project on the Economics of Higher Education, DP-24, May 1994.

2. A different set of issues would arise for, say, community colleges. For example, community college students are often taken unaware by placement exams they are given when they enroll. Failing to take the exam seriously, they then find that they must take extra courses to complete their degree because they are assigned to remedial sections. See James E. Rosenbaum and Lisbeth J. Goble, "What Do We Know about Succeeding in College? Questioning Our Assumptions about College Requirements," in *College Success: What It Means and How to Make It Happen*, ed. Michael McPherson and Morton Schapiro (New York: College Board, 2008).

merely a guidebook to the Ivy League, the advice here should apply to most four-year residential colleges in the United States that admit only a portion of applicants. To put a number on it, the advice should easily fit what the Princeton Review calls the country's 371 best colleges and probably a few hundred more besides.[3] The range is from Harvard to Angelo State, from Stanford to Lourdes.

What Universities Want

What are universities trying to do? To answer this question, you might start with their mission statements. The University of Miami's is "to educate and nurture students, to create knowledge, and to provide service to our community and beyond."[4] But what does this mission imply? It combines teaching, research, and service, three elements present in the mission statements of the sort of colleges described in this book. But how does the university carry them out, and how are they reconciled with each other?

One place to start understanding any organization is the bottom line: where the money comes from and where it goes.[5] But things are not so simple with universities because most of them are nonprofits. They are not simply trying to maximize their profits like Microsoft or General Electric. Any profits they earn have to be reinvested in the university, not distributed to owners or stockholders. So, universities are not out to get rich, or more precisely only wish to get rich to pursue other aims.

What are those other aims? The one aim that drives most colleges and universities, at least those discussed in this book, is a desire to increase their prestige. Universities wish to be viewed as the best in their line of work. They want to achieve the highest esteem among the general public and their peers that they can. To put it bluntly, everyone wants to be Harvard, and Harvard wants to make sure that no one else is Harvard.[6]

3. Princeton Review, *The Best 371 Colleges, 2010 Edition* (New York: Princeton Review, 2009).

4. See Burton A. Weisbrod, Jeffrey P. Ballou, and Evelyn D. Asch, *Mission and Money: Understanding the University* (Cambridge: Cambridge University Press, 2008), p. 64.

5. On this issue, see ibid.

6. A colleague of mine jokes that whenever he meets professors from a foreign university, they claim that their university is the Harvard of their country. He has already identified four Harvards of Canada.

Prestige of course is a zero-sum game. Only one university can be the best, only ten can be in the top ten, and so on down the line. If someone moves up, then someone else has to move down.[7] And so competition is fairly merciless.

Now the key question is where prestige comes from. The answer may be a surprise for some readers or immediately obvious to others. Universities and colleges are not viewed as prestigious because they provide the best undergraduate education or because they do the most for their students. Harvard is not Harvard because of what takes place in its classrooms. Truth be told, the classroom experience is more or less a black box for everyone but current students, and even they are in the dark to a certain extent.

Prestige comes, rather, from research. Universities are viewed as prestigious when they have the faculty that is most accomplished in scholarship. The most prestigious universities are the ones who employ the most Nobel Prize winners, the professors with the longest publishing records, and the scholars who are most frequently cited by their colleagues. It is excellence in research that puts Harvard, Yale, Stanford, and all the rest at the top of the heap and Podunk U at the bottom.

The Problem with Teaching

Why is it research excellence rather than teaching excellence that leads to prestige? Shouldn't it be the reverse? One important reason is that skill at teaching undergraduates is difficult to measure and compare. It is hard to determine who does teaching well and to what extent. Students are the main beneficiaries of good teaching, but they are not in a good position to compare universities (being as they attend only one) and are amateurs in the art of evaluation. Even university administrators find it difficult to evaluate their employees on this score since there is no gold standard of teaching, much less an objective way to measure it.

The outcomes of learning are also hard to quantify. There is no test administered to all graduating seniors to determine which universities did the

---

7. This is not to say that there cannot be absolute improvements in all universities. There can and have been. But prestige is a relative game. For a revealing description of how a university tries to move up the ladder, see Gaye Tuchman, *Wannabe U: Inside the Corporate University* (Chicago: University of Chicago Press, 2009).

best job educating their students. Career success is one standard, but it has its problems. Are Harvard graduates more successful because they learned more at Harvard or because Harvard was able to recruit the most talented students? As we shall see in the next chapter, it is mainly the latter.

Teaching quality is also less visible to the world at large. Professors, for example, have little idea who among their peers are the best teachers because they don't attend each others' classes or interact with students from other universities. And if professors who work day in and day out at the university don't know this, how are those outside the university supposed to find out? Because the benefits of teaching are felt locally, not globally, it is hard for them to increase a college's prestige. Prestige has to come from a factor that is visible beyond the university campus.

The Importance of Research

Now consider research, the task of coming up with new theories of how the world works. Excellence in research is easy to measure. Not only are there awards (the Nobel Prizes and their equivalents in each and every field), but there are publication records (numbers of books and journal articles), citation counts (how many times scholars are cited by others), and even confidential peer evaluations. These measures moreover are made by sophisticated experts rather than naive undergraduates. Most of us in a given field agree who the stars are and who the duds and which universities have more in each category.

Research similarly has a global reach. It is as visible across oceans and continents as it is on a single university campus. A scholar in London or Tokyo can easily pick up the latest article or monograph by a scholar from Omaha and judge for him- or herself its worth. And because all scholarship is produced by a community of scholars who read each other's work and build on what has gone before, they try to stay current on what is happening in their field.

Even the world at large values research over teaching. Consider who gets more respect in our society: the discoverers of new species, elementary particles, and medicines, or the teachers who get the most of their students? Whether you measure prestige by salaries, media attention, or simply pure admiration, research usually beats teaching. For all of these reasons, the prestige built on research is far more bankable than that built on teaching.

THE HISTORY OF THE UNIVERSITY

The roots of the modern university can be traced to the Middle Ages. The University of Bologna, often acknowledged as the first true university, was founded in the eleventh century and was soon followed by the University of Paris, Oxford University, and others. These schools taught a liberal arts curriculum—back then it consisted of grammar, logic, rhetoric, geometry, arithmetic, astronomy, and music—that was followed by vocational training in law, medicine, or theology. The faculty was itinerant (they moved around) and the student body cosmopolitan (they came from all over Europe).

The Protestant Reformation and the Catholic Counter-Reformation saw a decline in the academic content of these universities as they came to function more as defenders of the faith than of learning. The older American universities—like Harvard, Yale, and William and Mary—came out of this tradition. They were originally denominational schools whose mission was to train ministers and propagate the faith. As one college president of the time put it, only one book was needed in the library: the Bible.* The faculty of these universities could be called "ardent amateurs"† rather than trained specialists, and their job was to inculcate the revealed truth to their students.

Change to this model came not from within America but from across the ocean. The German universities of the nineteenth century heralded the birth of the sort of university we see today, centered on research and academic freedom.‡ The University of Berlin, founded by the philosopher Wilhelm von Humboldt, was at the center of these changes. The new curriculum would be based on objective, scientific truth rather than religious belief, and the professors would be specially trained in the methods necessary to conduct research. This style of university, sometimes called the research university, was first introduced to America by Johns Hopkins, but quickly expanded and now dominates higher educa-

---

*This was Mark Hopkins of Williams College.

†George Dennis O'Brien, *All the Essential Half-Truths about Higher Education* (Chicago: University of Chicago Press, 1998), p. 16.

‡On the birth of this sort of university, see William Clark, *Academic Charisma and the Origins of the Research University* (Chicago: University of Chicago Press, 2006).

tion; its ethos is present even at colleges where little original research takes place.§

Meanwhile the move to scientific knowledge meant that professors had to specialize in a particular field. Universities came to consist of distinct academic departments so that, as University of Chicago president Robert Hutchins put it, "The university is a collection of departments tied together by a common steam plant." Soon enough this specialization drifted down to the student level. In 1910, Harvard allowed students to choose their own concentration, and the modern academic major was born. Meanwhile, the common or core curriculum (the classics) gradually faded—retained at only a handful of schools—and was replaced by general education or distributional requirements. From the seven liberal arts, universities began to add courses in modern languages and literatures, the basic sciences, and the emerging social sciences (sociology, economics, political science, and anthropology). On the faculty side of things, the early part of the century saw the introduction of tenure, which was intended to allow professors to pursue politically incorrect or even heretical ideas in their research without fear for their jobs.

The significant changes to occur after this time were mainly in expanding both the student body and the course of education. Thus, state-sponsored land-grant institutions like the universities of Michigan, Minnesota, and Illinois emerged and opened their doors to a wider group of students—the less well-off, women, and minorities. (Quotas limiting these groups were standard practice at the major private universities at least through World War II if not longer.**) The curriculum expanded as well. The last forty years have seen the emergence of fields like women's studies, African American studies, and environmental studies along with new vocational fields tied to the needs of a changing economy. Universities have also made themselves more friendly to their new student body through better orientation and advising as well as more attention from faculty and more forthright attempts to deal with this new diversity.

§ The classic studies of the history of the university in America are Laurence Veysey, *The Emergence of the American University* (Chicago: University of Chicago Press, 1963), and Frederick Rudolph, *Curriculum: A History of the American Course of Study since 1636* (San Francisco: Jossey-Bass, 1977).

** See Jerome Karabel, *The Chosen: The Hidden History of Admission and Exclusion at Harvard, Yale, and Princeton* (Boston: Houghton Mifflin Harcourt, 2005).

How to Win the Prestige Game

So, for a university to become more prestigious—which is what its administrators, board, alumni, and probably even students want—it needs to hire scholars who are productive researchers. This may mean cherry-picking established scholars from other schools or trying to identify the bright young scholars from among newly minted PhDs.

How can schools attract these academic superstars (yes, that is what we call them)? Higher salaries help, but that is not what particularly motivates most professors. If they cared mainly about money, they would have chosen another profession.[8] Instead, professors also play the prestige game. They want to be esteemed in their field and, as in the university prestige game, research matters and for most of the same reasons. To win prestige they need to be turning out new articles and books as fast as they can.

To do this they need time to devote to research. Thus, when a university wishes to hire a superstar or potential superstar, the professor in question will negotiate to get more time to do her research, time that she can dispose of as she sees fit (otherwise known as discretionary time). This time almost always comes at the expense of teaching. After all, professors' main tasks are teaching and research.[9] Professors with good publishing records bargain for reduced teaching loads so that they can devote more time to research.

Since universities are competing with each other for the best scholars, they offer more discretionary time to the ones who are the most productive. If universities tried to force these productive scholars to spend more energy on teaching, they would lose them to other universities who would be glad to let Nobel Prize winners do whatever they want as long as they wear the university colors on graduation day. If you want to know why the famous

---

8. The average starting salary for an assistant professor is around $50,000–$60,000. The average full professor earns about $80,000–$110,000. The numbers are somewhat higher at major research universities and lower at less prestigious schools. Disciplines where faculty have better private sector alternatives—like economics and certain sciences—tend to pay more. For more details see the *Annual Report on the Economic Status of the Profession* published by the American Association of University Professors, available at www.aaup.org. The highest salaries for regular faculty members—this is, not presidents, coaches, and star physicians—are in the $300,000 range, and they are not common.

9. We do have other duties. Universities are self-governing, and so there are hundreds of committees on which we have to serve and thousands of meetings we have to attend.

professors at your university don't show up in the classroom very much, this is the answer.

Incentives and Teaching

It is not just discretionary time—which simply pulls professors out of the classroom—that matters for teaching quality. Having hired talented researchers, universities need to make sure that they have incentives to do as much high quality research as they can. For this reason, most of the rewards a professor can receive are for research success. Professors gain little—not salary, free time, or promotion—by becoming better teachers. They gain all of these things by becoming better researchers. Indeed, this incentive system was devised precisely in order to encourage more and better research and increase a university's prestige. If a professor has to decide where to allocate a free hour during the day, a simple cost-benefit analysis tells him or her that it should be spent on research rather than teaching.

Research is not the only thing that skews attention away from the classroom. A surprising fact is that most professors produce relatively little original research. The difficulties in measuring and evaluating teaching make it hard for universities to reward professors for better teaching even if they wanted to. Professors may be sanctioned for ignoring their classes, but it is difficult to identify and encourage exceptional effort. Developing an innovative course and spending extra time with students aren't easily monitored aspects of a professor's career.

At the same time, professors are not trained in the arts of teaching and tend to be suspicious of pedagogy.[10] They earned their PhDs in specific disciplines like anthropology or physics, not in teaching anthropology or teaching physics. One survey found that only 8 percent of professors have taken advantage of research on teaching methods.[11] Most professors are interested in the subject matter of their classes more than the best ways to teach it and so they do not actively pursue better ways of teaching. This would after all require extra effort for which they would not reap rewards. How many employees in any industry go the extra mile out of the goodness of their hearts?

10. University pedagogy continues to be a woefully underresearched subject.

11. Derek Bok, *Our Underachieving Colleges: A Candid Look at How Much Students Learn and Why They Should Be Learning More* (Princeton, NJ: Princeton University Press, 2006), p. 50.

The Undergraduate Connection

But where do undergraduates fit into the picture? After all, undergraduate dollars—first as tuition, later as alumni donations—fund most of this scheme. Why don't students choose universities that focus more energy on undergraduates and provide higher quality teaching? Why isn't the customer king as he is in restaurants, supermarkets, and clothing stores?

In the first place, it is hard for students to assess teaching quality, particularly at the level of an entire university. This is due to all the informational difficulties I mentioned earlier. Potential students and even rating agencies like *U.S. News* are not well placed to evaluate which schools provide the best education, partially because a great education is so intangible. Students therefore choose their universities based on clear variables like prestige rather than fuzzy ones like teaching quality.

It is not even clear that students are looking for teaching excellence. The demand for a great education is not as strong as you might think. Undergraduates are as hungry for prestige as everyone else. Even if Harvard professors completely ignored undergraduates but were the smartest guys in the world, they would still attract students. Many students do not see university primarily as a place to get the best possible education, but as a place to get a valuable credential (their diploma) that can be converted into a high-paying job. The credential is obviously worth more if it comes from a university considered prestigious.

Other students don't demand a better educational experience because they consider college mainly a nice place to while away four years before they start work, hence all of the money spent by universities on amenities like catered food, manicured lawns, luxurious (or at least fairly nice) dormitories, and entertaining sports teams. In many ways, universities have come to resemble country clubs complete with the requisite price tag. So long as life is pleasant outside the classroom and not too demanding inside, many students are content.

As far as education goes, universities only have to satisfy the minority of students who care about a great education. They thus put in place institutions that can be accessed by a few ambitious students but pass unnoticed by others. These institutions are not always highlighted because they would become prohibitively expensive if all students took advantage of them. One of the main aims of this book is to introduce you to these options.

Alumni, whose support and donations help the university to survive, generally share the desire of university administrators to maximize the university's prestige. How does great teaching help them? Their academic careers are long behind them. Greater prestige, by contrast, raises the value of their diploma as they become associated with a more prestigious brand. Alumni are also in a poor position to monitor the quality of an undergraduate education even if they wanted to; like everyone else, they have to rely on externally visible variables like research productivity, Nobel Prizes, and U.S. News rankings. If you want to see how universities try to impress their alumni, take a look at the opulent festivities during reunion weekend.[12]

12. The admissions process is also geared toward alumni. A recent study found that alumni increased their donations as their kids approached college age and rewarded the college with higher donations for admitting their children and cut them off for nonadmission. Colleges therefore have strong financial incentives to admit legacies. See Jonathan Meer and Harvey S. Rosen, "Altruism and the Child-Cycle of Alumni Giving," NBER Working Paper 13152, June 2007.

A STUDENT'S GUIDE TO COLLEGE ADMINISTRATION

Most of your nonstudent contacts at college will be with ordinary teaching professors. But universities also have a large administrative apparatus that sits above them. While it is not worth your while to spend much time thinking about this group of people, there may be a few situations where they can be helpful. In particular, presidents, provosts, and deans are often on the lookout for new ideas and initiatives that they can show to donors as evidence of their good work. These ideas are fairly rare, but if you have one—for example, you want to put together a new charitable program or an international learning initiative—consider getting in touch with administrators.* Besides that, here is what you need to know about the administration.

President. The university president is more or less a fundraiser and a cheerleader for the university.† Yes, creative and astute presidents can put forth major initiatives and sometimes even see them through

* Almost all of these officials were also once professors and so may be helpful if you work in their field, but beware that their time is extremely limited.

† As one former president puts it, "After my first year as a president, I had presided at so many dedications and welcoming ceremonies that I decided that what was needed was not a president, but a Prince of Wales—a non-authoritative, but impressive official greeter." See George Dennis O'Brien, All the Essential Half-Truths about Higher Education (Chicago:, University of Chicago Press, 1998), p. 116.

to completion, but their main role is to be visible representatives of the university to the world at large and especially to the university's main donors.‡ It may be nice to shake the hand of the president of your university—make sure to snap a picture because it probably won't happen again—but other than that he or she will play very little role in your life.

Provost. It is said that real power in a university rests with the provost who is the chief academic officer, making day-to-day decisions on policy. Because provosts hold the purse strings, they are said to have de facto control over university policy. There are rarely reasons for you to get to know the provost, and even faculty view them as slightly ominous figures. Just about the only reason a professor will become provost is because they view it as a stepping stone to becoming president.

Deans. Universities usually have a variety of deans with different responsibilities: academic affairs, faculty affairs, graduate affairs, and so on. Some deans are regular faculty members who are doing "service" to the university for a limited length of time, while others have taken the job on a semi-permanent basis. The job offers them perks like a higher salary and time off from teaching, but also its share of politicking. Deans make most of the student-level policy decisions at the university—like granting medical leaves, adjudicating cases of plagiarism, etc.—and may be useful if you have issues that are impeding your academic progress or personal well-being. Outside of helping solve these problems—whose resolution take up most of a dean's time—deans do not have a lot to offer to you. Some places where they may be positively useful (rather than just helping you out of trouble) are if you want to pursue an innovative academic program that is not on the books or create a new student organization.

Department chair. Like deans, most department chairs take the post out of a sense of duty and serve limited terms (often of three years). They spend most of their day dealing with the complaints of their own colleagues—yes, we do complain a lot—and so are relatively inaccessible to students. The work of interacting with students and solving their problems in the department is usually delegated to regular teaching fac-

‡ As two scholars put it, the role of a university president is like that of a driver trying to control a car in a skid. More generally, they refer to university administration as "organized anarchy." See Michael D. Cohen and James G. March, *Leadership and Ambiguity: The American College President* (New York: Harvard Business School Press, 1986).

ulty with more general issues devolving to a director of undergraduate studies. In any case, chairs have relatively few means at their disposal to personally advance your education. They should thus be approached mainly if you are interested in the topics they study, though even then expect a brush-off because most of their time is spent dealing with administrative matters. Chairs may also be a useful first contact if you have suggestions for improving their department like offering more courses in a certain area or bringing in specific outside speakers.

Cause for Hope

While this assessment may seem excessively gloomy, there is hope. Universities have actually been getting better over time at both research and teaching. It was once the case that universities did not compete for students; graduates of Andover and other prep schools went to the Ivy League universities, while everyone else went to their local public university. And in the not too distant past, students did not demand that professors devote time and effort to their education. Many were content to listen passively to a distinguished lecturer and take their gentlemen's C. College was more a finishing school than a place of learning.

Today this is no longer the case. Universities compete hard for the best students, and students demand more faculty involvement. This has led universities to emphasize classroom teaching more than they once did. Popular criticism of an out-of-touch professoriate has had the same effect. A number of recent books decrying the decline of undergraduate teaching have embarrassed universities and led them to put more resources into their educational mission.[13] Because so much of their funding comes directly or indirectly from the government, universities are keen to remain in the good graces of politicians. This means, among other things, maintaining a pristine public image.

The upshot, as former Harvard president Derek Bok puts it, is that "colleges launched a variety of experiments to provide more individualized in-

13. See Charles Sykes, *Profscam: Professors and the Demise of Higher Education* (New York: St. Martin's Press, 1988), and Richard M. Huber, *How Professors Play the Cat Guarding the Cream: Why We're Paying More and Getting Less in Higher Education* (Fairfax, VA: George Mason University Press, 1992).

struction, at least for portions of the student body. Honors programs were established for qualified students. Research internships offered opportunities for undergraduates to work in laboratories alongside experienced investigators. Freshman seminars, group tutorials, and small senior colloquia afforded students at least a modicum of personal contact with faculty members."[14]

Evidence that something has changed can be found in a recent survey of college graduates that asked whether they had received special attention from faculty members during their college career. Graduates from the late eighties were far more likely to report that they had received special attention than those who graduated in the mid-seventies or mid-fifties.[15] The trend is toward better teaching and more personal attention, especially for those who seek it out.

Has this trend also diminished research productivity? Not at all. Professors are far more productive today than they once were (and there are more of us doing research). The reason is that they are working more hours than they used to—at least that is my sense with all due respect to my senior colleagues—and they have better technologies for doing research. They no longer have to create punch cards and queue for time on a computer or send their paper drafts to collaborators by snail mail.

I would be remiss if I didn't mention that most professors are conscientious about their teaching, even if they lack strong incentives to be conscientious. They do feel an obligation to their students. Moreover, teaching does provide intrinsic satisfactions. It gratifies us when students like our classes and depresses us when they do not. Most of us see teaching undergraduates as a public service that we are happy to provide, particularly when students want to learn.

In sum, the modern American university is built to maximize its prestige, which comes from employing scholars who produce original research. Universities compete with each other for these researchers and spend most of their discretionary resources trying to attract them and induce them to do more and better research. Undergraduate education takes second place to this dynamic, not necessarily because universities want it to—they would

14. Bok, *Our Underachieving Colleges*, p. 20.

15. George R. Goethals, Laurie C. Hurshman, Adam C. Sischy, Gordon C. Winston, Georgi Zhelev, and David J. Zimmerman, "Who Cares? How Students View Faculty and Other Adults in Higher Education," Williams Project on the Economics of Higher Education, DP-67, 2004.

surely like to provide great teaching—but because they would lose prestige by putting it first. But things are getting better as universities increasingly find themselves under pressure to improve teaching quality, and many appear to be doing so. The tips that follow will show you how to take advantage of these changes.

 Choosing a College

Choosing a college may be the first "adult" decision that most readers of this book will make or have already made. Unfortunately, I am going to take a little of the air out of what seems like an incredibly difficult and consequential decision.[1] To a large degree your choice of university—at least within a large class of selective four-year institutions—does not matter very much. Not only are most students satisfied with their choice, but in important respects most colleges are pretty much alike.

While universities do differ in certain ways, the classroom experience is not one of the main ones. Teaching and learning occur in more or less the same ways at all colleges. Economics 101 and Chemistry 101 are virtually the same course at both Podunk U and Harvard and may even be of lower quality at more prestigious universities.

Nevertheless, there are some significant differences between universities that may make one or another a better fit for you. The main choice for academically minded students is between large research-oriented universities and small teaching-oriented colleges, though recently even this distinction has been blurred. Unless your dad is Bill Gates, cost should probably play a role in your calculations, and even some more superficial factors like location may be important as well. However, as far as academic programs go, distinctions—with a few exceptions—are more apparent than real.

1. On the other hand, it is hard to shake the impression that students decide fairly arbitrarily. Many eliminate colleges because their tour guide was a flake or the basketball team was having a bad year.

TIP 1

....

You Can Get an Equivalent Classroom Education at Most Reasonably Selective Colleges and Universities

There are two reasons why the educational experience is more or less the same across American universities. The first was described in the previous chapter. Universities do not have good means to monitor teaching quality, much less provide professors with incentives to do a better job at teaching. It is simply hard to tell if particular professors are doing a good job in the classroom and therefore it is hard to motivate them to do a better job. And because teaching quality is difficult to sell to the world at large—who verifies that one college does it better than others?—colleges tend not to encourage it. Professors do not earn large rewards—promotions or raises—for great classroom performance and so do not always give it their all. In fact, faculty at higher-ranked universities are under less pressure to teach well simply because they are under greater pressure to do research. As you go down the academic hierarchy, the emphasis on teaching actually goes up.

The second reason the classroom experience is so homogeneous has to do with the way professors are trained. Most professors learned their trade at the same handful of doctoral-granting institutions. More to the point, virtually all of them earned degrees in specific disciplines that emphasize certain core methods and results. Put together a group of physicists or sociologists and you will find that they have read most of the same books and articles and profess the same basic theories.[2]

This sort of standardized training has led to a standardized educational experience. First off, just about all colleges are divided into the same academic departments—art history, geology, psychology, etc.—because professors received their doctorates in those fields. And because their training was similar, course offerings are more or less the same. An economics major almost always begins with an introductory course followed by intermediate

2. This process of standardization is called the professionalization of a particular field. It is a good thing in that it allows scholars to communicate and build on each other's work; it can be worrisome if it squeezes out unpopular ideas. A similar process has taken place in fields like medicine and law. For an example of how this standardization happened in the discipline of history, see Peter Novick, *That Noble Dream: "The Objectivity Question" and the American Historical Profession* (Cambridge: Cambridge University Press, 1988).

macro and micro; chemistry departments usually start with two semesters of inorganic chemistry followed by two semesters of organic chemistry; no English major is complete without courses in Shakespeare and the nineteenth-century novel. Needless to say, it is not just the course titles that resemble each other, but the actual content. For years, every Econ 101 course worth its salt used Paul Samuelson's famous textbook; even today a handful of textbooks dominate in most fields that use them.

Yes, there are differences. As you move to upper-division courses, you will find variety that reflects professors' specialties, and you will find greater variety at larger universities simply because they employ more professors. At less prestigious universities meanwhile, professors may dilute the material in introductory courses to accommodate weaker students (though they may also offer "go faster, do more" versions of these same courses). And lower-ranked universities may feature some departments that are academically suspect in order to cater to less motivated students. It is, however, easy enough to avoid this less rigorous education.

It is not just the content of classes that is similar across universities; it is their style. It is the rare professor who has any formal training in the art of teaching. Our graduate training focused entirely on learning our field, not how to teach it to undergraduates. We received our doctorates for producing original research, not for becoming skilled teachers. Almost all of us are teaching amateurs who have learned to catch as catch can. Because there is little incentive to be innovative, we have mostly stuck to the tried and true like the standard lecture format or the midterm/final form of evaluation. In short, the classroom experience is similar at most universities in terms of professors' commitment, course content, and teaching styles.

This conclusion may be hard for you to stomach; after all, everyone knows that Harvard is better than Podunk U. Let me back it up with some hard evidence. For the last several years, scholars have surveyed tens of thousands of students at over a thousand colleges and universities across the United States. They asked students about the degree of academic challenge, active and collaborative learning, student-faculty interaction, enriching educational experiences, and a supportive environment at their colleges. These are all the things you should be getting out of college. The results were striking. Let me first quote from the latest report, "NSSE [the National Survey of Student Engagement] has found that students attending the same institution differ from each other a lot more than the average student at that institution differs from those at other institutions."[3] What this means is that the educational experiences of Harvard students differ more from each other than a typical student at Harvard differs from a typical student at Podunk U. And the difference is enormous. When comparing the degree to which students felt challenged or interacted with faculty, only 4 to 8 percent of the variation could be attributed to whether they attended Harvard or Podunk U. The rest—over 90 percent of the differences—was among students within institutions.

Or consider the conclusion of two researchers who reviewed hundreds of studies on the effects of universities: "on just about any outcome, and after taking account of the characteristics of the students enrolled, the dimensions along which American colleges are typically categorized, ranked, and studied, such as type of control, size, and selectivity, are simply not linked with important differences in student learning, change, or development."[4] As I said in the introduction, the difference is not between colleges, it is between students who suck the juice out of them and those who don't. Universities are more or less the same. What is different is what students take away from them. The following chapters will show you how to get more out of whatever school you choose.

3. National Survey of Student Engagement, *Promoting Engagement for All Students: The Imperative to Look Within: 2008 Results*, Indiana University Center for Postsecondary Research, www.nsse.iub.edu, p. 12.

4. Ernest T. Pascarella and Patrick T. Terenzini, *How College Affects Students*, vol. 2, *A Third Decade of Research* (San Francisco: Jossey-Bass, 2005), p. 641.

NOBEL PRIZE WINNERS

In his book *Outliers*, Malcolm Gladwell tries to explain why certain people become enormously successful. What makes an ordinary smart kid into a Bill Gates? One explanation that he considers and then dismisses is where they went to college. Consider the last twenty-five Americans to win the Nobel Prize in Chemistry and the Nobel Prize in Medicine, two of the highest marks of success a person can achieve. You might expect that most of the winners would be graduates of Harvard, Yale, and Princeton.

In fact, of those fifty winners, more than half went to colleges that wouldn't be viewed as the most prestigious. These included large state schools like the Universities of Florida, Illinois, Massachusetts, Minnesota, Nebraska, North Carolina, Texas, and Washington as well as smaller and lesser known schools like Augsburg, Antioch, Dayton, DePauw, Gettysburg, Holy Cross, Hope, and Rollins. And this probably overstates the influence of the Harvards of the world, which not only have more resources for teaching, but admit the cream of each year's high school crop. In short, don't worry about attending one of the very top schools. You can be a success anywhere.* After all, Bill Gates went to Harvard, but he also dropped out.

---

* According to Gladwell, the roots of success are elsewhere, particularly in a person's willingness to work hard—you need to devote ten thousand hours to your chosen activity to become a true expert—and chance factors like when and where you were born. See Malcolm Gladwell, *Outliers: The Story of Success* (New York: Little, Brown and Company, 2008), pp. 81–83

TIP 2

The Key Distinction Is between Small Colleges and Large Universities

From the point of view of teaching, the key difference between colleges is whether they are large research-oriented universities or small teaching-oriented colleges.[5] At both kinds you can get a great education. However, the accessibility and style of the education differ. Whether you choose one or the other depends on the type of person you are. Some types will thrive at large research universities; others will do better at small colleges. Let me explain.

Large research universities do three things, only one of which is educating undergraduates. The other two are producing research and training graduate students. In some ways these activities are complementary: professors who are at the cutting edge of research know their fields very well (in addition to being very smart) and so can teach undergraduates the most up-to-date knowledge and provide the best answers to their questions. But there are also trade-offs: because professors are hired for their research productivity and expected to continually produce original research, they may not be great teachers and have much less incentive to devote extra time to their teaching. Some of them view teaching undergraduates as a distraction from their "real" work.

5. I will use the words "university" and "college" interchangeably in this book, but technically university refers to a school that offers both graduate and undergraduate degrees, while a college only offers undergraduate degrees.

The mission of these universities to train future professors probably falls more on the trade-off side. A good proportion of your interaction with instructors at these schools will be with graduate students who grade most papers and exams, lead discussion sections, and sometimes teach their own courses. This does not necessarily have to detract from your education. Graduate students are young, hardworking, and more accessible than full-time faculty. (And without them there would be no professors in the future, much less new knowledge.) But they know their fields less well, are less experienced teachers than professors, and have their own research to worry about—their main task is writing a doctoral dissertation.[6]

I do not intend this as a negative judgment of research universities. If you are sufficiently proactive and ambitious, you will find in them the best possible education the world has to offer. As the Harvard economist Greg Mankiw puts it, "For someone who wants to consider a research career, being at a top research school conveys significant benefits: You get to know more active researchers early on, and you can attend a large array of research seminars. But those opportunities are not relevant for 90 percent of students at these schools, who will not go on to become PhD economerds but will instead become doctors, lawyers, corporate executives, and so on."[7]

To get the best education at such a university, you have to be a go-getter. You have to make yourself known to the full-time faculty. You have to show them that you are worth taking seriously, that you care about their field and have numerous talents. If you can do this, professors will take you under their wing, show you how their field works at the highest level, and perhaps even help you produce your own original work.

If you are shy and lack self-confidence, however, you may lose some of the benefits such universities offer. Indeed, most students at these schools do not get involved in the research atmosphere, much less form bonds with professors. Instead, they end up taking mostly large lecture courses and interacting primarily with graduate students. While some of these classes will be life-changing experiences, few instructors will take you seriously as an individual. Most students at these universities become a face in the crowd,

---

6. In some fields, a good proportion of graduate students are from abroad. This leads to the common complaint that they do not speak English well. This is sometimes true, though universities have become more careful in monitoring their knowledge of English. On the plus side, they provide a fresh perspective on our country.

7. See Greg Mankiw, "On Choosing a College," gregmankiw.blogspot.com.

particularly in the larger and more popular majors (see Tip 39). If you do not seek out your professors, they usually will not seek you out.

What does a small teaching-oriented college offer? In many ways it is the opposite of the research university. There are no graduate students. Almost all of the classes are taught by professors. Many more, probably most, of them will be small seminars. You will likely get to know many of your professors personally or at least have the opportunity to do so. You will probably meet them walking around campus since these schools are often in small towns. And your professors will return the favor. They will learn your name and something about you. They are not required to do as much research and are encouraged to be good teachers. In fact, many of them end up at such schools precisely because they enjoy teaching and are good at it.[8]

One of the surveys of college graduates that I referred to earlier confirms this impression. The survey asked students whether during their undergraduate studies anyone other than fellow students took "a special interest" in their work, whether there "was someone you could turn to for advice or for general support or encouragement." At small liberal arts colleges, 62 percent of students answered that a faculty member took an interest in them versus 36 percent for public research universities and 41 percent for private research universities.[9] Incidentally, Ivy League schools came in near the bottom with 37 percent.[10]

A small college is perfect for you if you are less confident in your abilities and lack the moxie to draw attention to yourself. This is not to say that you are less talented. Only that you would thrive more in an environment where you are a big fish in a small pond. Indeed, there is a less competitive atmosphere at such schools. You are less likely to have to compete with the

8. A survey of professors found that 63 percent of professors at liberal arts colleges believed that "teaching effectiveness should be the primary criterion for promoting faculty." By contrast, 69 percent of faculty at research universities said that it should "not" be the primary criterion. The percentage who viewed research as an essential job responsibility was almost identical: 90 percent versus 94 percent. See Robert A. McCaughey, *Scholars and Teachers: The Faculty of Select Liberal Arts Colleges and Their Place in American Higher Education* (New York: Mellon Foundation, 1994).

9. George R. Goethals, Laurie C. Hurshman, Adam C. Sischy, Gordon C. Winston, Georgi Zhelev, and David J. Zimmerman, "Who Cares? How Students View Faculty and Other Adults in Higher Education," Williams Project on the Economics of Higher Education, DP-67, 2004.

10. For all schools, the percentage of faculty taking a special interest has increased over time suggesting that higher education has become more not less personalized.

superstars who have been trained since the age of two to attend Harvard and who draw all of the professors' attention to themselves.

What could be wrong with such a picture? The main thing that is missing is contact with the cutting edge of research. Fewer professors at small colleges are doing major work in the field; there are fewer geniuses around.[11] And the university as a whole is less geared to research—that means fewer public lectures and conferences, less money to build labs or travel to foreign countries. This may not be noticeable for most undergraduates, but for the very top students to whom this book is addressed, there are fewer opportunities at such schools. A final black mark against these schools is that they are almost all private and hence expensive, though most do offer significant financial aid.[12]

I would add, however, that these small teaching-oriented colleges produce more future professors—a higher percentage of their students go on to get PhDs.[13] The reason I think is that students at these schools tend to identify with their professors much more and can see themselves following in their footsteps. For most students at research-oriented universities, the professoriate is a distant and mysterious group.

Note that what I have set out here is a contrast of ideal types—the difference between the prototypical large research-oriented university and the prototypical small teaching-oriented college. In fact, over the past twenty or so years these distinctions have been breaking down. Large universities have started to offer more college-type experiences with smaller seminars and greater contact with faculty (though they have not forsaken research or graduate students). Some offer special honors programs or liberal arts colleges embedded within the university. Conversely, small colleges have begun to require a much greater research commitment from faculty. Differences between the two types may thus be on the decline, but they still exist.

The takeaway point for you is to determine whether you have the self-confidence and talent to take advantage of the resources of a large research

11. When asked by Senator George McGovern what the difference between an education at Harvard and one at Wellesley was, the economist John Kenneth Galbraith replied, "Well, at Harvard, if you're lucky, you might get Galbraith once a week. At Wellesley, you might get one of my C-minus students three days a week." The quip is unfair to Wellesley.

12. There are a handful of public liberal arts colleges like the University of Minnesota, Morris.

13. See, for example, Joan Burrelli, Alan Rapoport, and Rolf Lehming, "Baccalaureate Origins of S&E Doctoral Recipients," National Science Foundation, Discussion Paper NSF 08-311, July 2008.

university or whether you need personal attention to be more accessible
and competition less cutthroat. To put it more bluntly than I should, do you
want the floor of the New York Stock Exchange where fortunes are made
by those with the talent to succeed or a greenhouse where gardeners tend
to all of their plants?

WHERE DO PROFESSORS SEND THEIR CHILDREN TO COLLEGE?

The main difficulty in choosing a college is information. How can you
know what you are buying with your tuition dollars until you actually
enroll at a college?* While many guidebooks try to provide you with
information, it is hard to produce a simple and accurate evaluation of
such an intangible and multidimensional experience as a university education; colleges are not toaster ovens.

One way to get a more accurate sense of quality is to consider the
choices that insiders make. Insiders are people who work inside an institution. In any field, insiders know their institutions better than anyone
else and thus have the information to make the best choices in matters concerning them. You would expect, for example, that stockbrokers
would make wiser investment choices than their customers, and it turns
out that they do.† And real estate agents receive higher prices for their
homes than their clients do.‡

In evaluating colleges, the consummate insiders are professors. They
have been trained at universities, spent their lives working at them, and
have close friends at universities across the country. You would expect
them to know the right places to send their kids—which colleges and
universities will give their kids the best education and set them on the
right path.

It turns out that if you compare the college choices of children of

---

* In this respect, choosing a college is much like buying a used car but with fewer
lemons.

† In fact, U.S. congressmen also make better investment choices than others; they
beat the market by 12 percent a year. Ask yourself why that is. See James Surowiecki,
"Capitol Gains," *New Yorker*, October 31, 2005. The original research is by Georgia
State professor Alan Ziobrowski.

‡ Stephen J. Dubner and Steven D. Levitt, *Freakonomics: A Rogue Economist Ex-
plores the Hidden Side of Everything* (New York: William Morrow, 2005).

university faculty and those of equivalent nonfaculty, you see large differences.§ The accompanying table shows the universities where professors most commonly send their children. Professors are far more likely to send their children to small liberal arts colleges and somewhat more likely to send them to major research universities than other parents. This holds even when you look at parents with similar incomes and educational attainments. Children of university faculty are about twice as likely to attend small liberal arts colleges as children of families earning more than $100,000 a year who you would expect to be well informed on such matters and not particularly worried about the cost.

This difference is telling. If your stockbroker told you which stocks he had in his own portfolio, you would probably buy them. If university faculty are telling you that they think liberal arts colleges are the best place for their children, then you may want to heed their advice.

The Most Popular Colleges for Children of Professors
(from a survey of 5,592 students)

1. Oberlin College: 61	5. University of Michigan, Ann
2. Carleton College: 36	Arbor: 27
3. Stanford University: 36	6. University of Chicago: 26
4. Duke University: 33	

---

§ John Siegfried and Malcolm Getz, "Where Do the Children of Professors Attend College?" *Economics of Education Review* 25, no. 2 (2006): 201–10.

TIP 3

Reputation Doesn't Matter as Much as You Think

Most Americans could easily reel off the names of the "best" or most prestigious universities. The answers are so obvious that I do not need to list them here. But are these the places where you can get the best education? The very fact that they are consistently at the top of the rankings suggests that they are not. If rankings of colleges were truly based on the quality of education they offer, then we would probably expect some changes over time. Are we to believe that Harvard, Yale, and Princeton (there, I've said their names) consistently offer the best education? Perhaps. But the consistency of the ratings suggests that something else is at work.

The reputation of these universities is not earned through detailed studies of the sort of education they provide and whether their students are learning more than at other schools. Indeed, nobody really knows how to measure an education. Rather, their reputations come from comparisons of the sort of students and faculty they attract. Their students have higher SAT scores, their faculty publish more, and they have more money to spend on both.[14] Students and faculty in turn are attracted by the reputation and money, which is in turn a consequence of the students and faculty. You see where I am heading here.

You might object that even if Harvard is not providing a better education, a Harvard diploma does impress employers and graduate schools and thus leads to more success. Indeed, graduates of more highly rated schools do earn higher salaries; a college with one hundred point higher average SAT scores will produce graduates who earn 3 to 7 percent higher wages.[15] But is this difference due to the better education that Harvard students receive or the fact that Harvard admits more talented students (and provides them with better connections)? It is hard to distinguish these effects.

Two researchers, however, discovered a way to separate the effects of precollege talent and learning that takes place at college.[16] Their trick was to compare students who were admitted to the same colleges and universities, but some of whom chose to matriculate at the more selective schools and others at less selective schools. It turned out that these similar students had the same success on the job market. Students who were admitted to Harvard but went to State U instead earned the same salaries as comparable students who did go to Harvard. The supposedly better education at the more selective schools did not give students an advantage once their precollege talents were controlled for. Or as a senior dean at one major university put it, we "admit good students and then make a special effort to 'get out of their way.'"[17]

14. A recent study, however, found that their advantages in research productivity have been declining. See E. Han Kim, Adair Morse, and Luigi Zingales, "Are Elite Universities Losing Their Competitive Edge?" NBER Working Paper 12245, May 2006.

15. Thomas Kane, "Racial and Ethnic Preferences in College Admissions," in *The Black-White Test Score Gap*, ed., Christopher Jencks and Meredith Phillips (Washington, DC: Brookings Institute, 1998).

16. Stacy Berg Dale and Alan Krueger, "Estimating the Payoff to Attending a More Selective College: An Application of Selection on Observables and Unobservables," *Quarterly Journal of Economics* 117, no. 4 (2002): 1491–1527.

17. Richard J. Light, *Making the Most of College: Students Speak Their Minds* (Cambridge, MA: Harvard University Press, 2001), p. 2.

TIP 4
....

The Main Importance of Reputation Is
the Student Body It Attracts

Reputation does have its effects. Higher-ranked schools attract more impressive students. Does this matter for you? Some research has found significant peer effects in education.[18] That is, you learn more or less depending on who your fellow students are. While much of this research has focused on elementary and high schools, new work has found such peer effects at universities as well.

Several studies have looked at the effects of one's freshman year roommate. Since roommates are assigned randomly, the process resembles a lab experiment; you can compare students who got good and bad roommates. These studies have found that students of middling achievement (measured by SAT scores) did worse academically when they roomed with low-achieving students and better with high-achieving students. (High- and low-achieving students, however, were mostly unaffected by their environment.) This is not surprising. Being around smart and studious people is likely to rub off. Indeed, this is one of the reasons why selective universities try to maintain high admission standards.

More generally, one can imagine that seminar and dorm room discussions are more intense where brighter, harder-working students are participating in them. Being surrounded by other students devoted to learning should nurture those same desires in less motivated students. This is not to say that a smart, ambitious student will be lost at a less selective college. Even at the biggest party schools, one can find peers who are smart and care about learning. Similarly, even highly selective schools have less academic subcultures. On average, though, the student body will help you to get a better education at a more selective school. This appears to be particularly important for students from disadvantaged backgrounds like many ethnic minorities (see the text box on "Minorities and College Choice").

18. See, for example, Bruce Sacerdote, "Peer Effects with Random Assignment: Results for Dartmouth Roommates," *Quarterly Journal of Economics* 116 (2001); David J. Zimmerman, "Peer Effects in Academic Outcomes: Evidence from a Natural Experiment," Williams Project on the Economics of Higher Education, DP-52, 1999; and George Goethals, Gordon Winston, and David Zimmerman, "Students Educating Students: The Emerging Roles of Peer Effects in Higher Education," Williams Project on the Economics of Higher Education, DP-50, 1999. The effects seem to be weaker at less selective schools.

U.S. NEWS RATINGS

What should you make of the *U.S. News* ratings of colleges and universities? Everybody looks at them; even professors take a gander every now and then. Are the ratings at all meaningful? My view is that you can learn something from them, but that they should be taken with a very large grain of salt.

In the first place, the headline numbers—the number 1, 2, and 3 schools—are almost entirely deceiving. Every year *U.S. News* jiggers their formula in order to produce a new number 1 so that they can advertise the magazine.* The formulas are also fixed so that the same three schools—can you guess which?—always end up at the top. Indeed, the formula for calculating the headline numbers was manufactured not because it seemed to capture the best possible education, but because it led to these three schools occupying the top spots. (There was one year where they used a better formula, but Cal Tech came out on top and so the formula was discarded.) If you do decide to look at these headline numbers, then look at large blocks of colleges. Assume that there is little difference between numbers 1 and 20 or 30 and 50.

That said, you may find useful information in the components of the rankings rather than the headline score. *U.S. News* does provide a worthwhile function by gathering comparable information about a large number of schools. While some universities have complained that the *U.S. News* scores are misleading, they have not come up with a better way of getting comparable statistics into the hands of potential applicants. If universities wished, they could produce far better rankings themselves, but they choose not to do so.

What do the components of the ratings tell you? First of all, the peer assessment is based on a survey of the school's reputation. If you are after prestige, then follow this score. I mentioned earlier the possibility

* See Bruce Gottlieb, "Cooking the School Books: How *U.S. News* Cheats in Picking Its 'Best American Colleges,'" *Slate*, September 1, 1999; Nicholas Thompson, "Cooking the School Books (Yet Again): The *U.S. News* College Rankings Get Phonier and Phonier," *Slate*, September 15, 2000; Nicholas Thompson, "The Best, the Top, the Most," *New York Times*, August 3, 2003; Stuart Rojstaczer, "College Rankings Are Mostly about Money," *San Francisco Chronicle*, September 3, 2001. And for an alternative method, Paul Boyer, *College Rankings Exposed* (Lawrenceville, NJ: Thomson's Peterson, 2003).

that having smarter fellow students may improve your education. If you believe this, then look at the student selectivity measure—the percentage of applicants accepted and the average SAT scores of admitted students.

The faculty resources score will tell you something about how much attention you will get from faculty. It includes measures of average class size, student-faculty ratios, and the percentage of full-time faculty. The financial resources measure tells you how much money the university spends for its size. This will indicate the amount of resources potentially there for you, but it is biased in favor of large research universities, which devote enormous sums to scientific laboratories.

Unfortunately, universities have learned to game all of these scores and so they are somewhat less informative than they could be. Thus,

> to appear more selective, some institutions count incomplete applications as denials to lower the acceptance rate. (Students may have mailed the first part but never submitted test scores or high-school transcripts.) Other colleges defer admission to the second semester and then don't report those students as admitted to *U.S. News.* ... A number of colleges don't require the SAT exam but proudly report high average SAT scores, ignoring the obvious fact that when SATs are optional, only the highest scorers submit their scores. Others omit the SAT scores of international students or recruited athletes.†

All of these factors make even these component parts far from perfect.

If you are in the market for rankings of colleges, I would recommend instead those produced by the *Washington Monthly* (www .washingtonmonthly.com/college_guide), which asks whether particular universities are benefiting our country. They focus on three factors: social mobility (does the university recruit and graduate low income students), research (does the university produce cutting-edge research), and service (does the university encourage students to give back to the community), all of which are much harder for universities to manipulate. Interestingly, these ratings produce a far different picture than *U.S. News* with Jackson State outranking Yale and Utah State beating Princeton.

† See Michael S. McPherson and Morton Owen Schapiro, "Moral Reasoning and Higher-Education Policy," *Chronicle of Higher Education*, September 7, 2007.

MINORITIES AND COLLEGE CHOICE

I advised you in Tip 3 not to take college reputation too seriously. But there is an important exception to this rule. Minority students, especially ones from underprivileged backgrounds, should apply to and enroll in the most prestigious schools they can. Even if they feel their abilities are not up to snuff, they should let admissions committees make that call. If they have a choice between a major university like the University of Michigan, Ann Arbor and the less prestigious Western Michigan, they should choose the more prestigious one.

This advice might seem surprising. After all, some scholars have claimed that due to affirmative action minority students get mismatched to colleges that are too difficult for them and as a result have higher dropout rates.* In fact, a recent study of ninety-four thousand university students found just the opposite.† Minority students instead tend to be undermatched—they go to less prestigious schools than they could have. And the result of undermatching is lower completion rates. Minority students are more likely to finish college when they go to a more prestigious school even if they are underprepared going in.

The reason appears to be the culture of prestigious colleges (see Tip 4). Surrounded by other students who are intent on being successful, on working hard and finishing school, minority students adopt that culture. Conversely, at schools with high dropout rates and where many students take the experience less seriously, it is harder for underprepared students to succeed. If you come from an underprivileged background, then aim high in your choice of college.

* See Scott Jaschik, "Testing for 'Mismatch,'" *Inside Higher Ed*, April 20, 2009.
† William G. Bowen, Matthew M. Cingos, and Michael S. McPherson, *Crossing the Finish Line: Completing College at America's Public Universities* (Princeton, NJ: Princeton University Press, 2009).

TIP 5

Look for Signs of a Personalized Education

What a university should provide is an education that takes you seriously as an individual. Conventional rankings like those based on reputation, however, have a hard time capturing this. As the text box on the *U.S. News* rankings shows, even seemingly objective measures like student-faculty ratios can be manipulated. Your research on colleges should therefore focus on finding universities that do care about students as individuals. While there are no hard and fast rules for doing this nor good, objective measures of these factors, some of the things you should look for are

- A lot of small, seminar classes, particularly for underclassmen (see Tip 15). It is in such classes that you will get personal contact with professors and feedback on your work. Look out for a strong system of freshman as well as senior seminars.
- A strong writing program that offers multiple writing-intensive courses across different departments and continues for all four years of college (see Tip 14). Writing is one of the main skills you need to take away from college, and many colleges don't devote enough attention to it.
- An active residential life. Since much of your learning comes from interactions with your fellow students, it is important that they be around campus a lot. You will get less out of college if you and many of your fellow students live at home. A nice addition to many colleges is residential dorms organized around a particular topic or activity like public affairs or theater.
- Opportunities to participate in research. Research is one of the best ways of learning a field and extending your abilities. A good university should give you opportunities to pursue research in your courses and in collaboration with professors (see Tip 60).
- The opportunity to write a senior thesis or complete another capstone project. There should be a concluding exercise to your college career that both sums up what you have learned and challenges you to solve a difficult problem in your chosen field (see Tip 43).

You should also keep a look out for colleges that offer special honors programs or small colleges embedded within larger universities. Such programs allow you to get a great education even if many of your fellow students do not.

TIP 6
....
Consider the Cost

If colleges and universities are mainly the same, at least inside the classroom, how should you choose among them? One factor where they do differ is cost.

The price of college has been rising for years and at a rate much higher than inflation. The sticker price at the top universities now tops $40,000 a year. If you are lucky enough to have rich parents, this isn't a problem. But for others, it means that you either forgo college altogether or take out student loans. The median graduate now leaves college $20,000 in debt. The economic benefits of a college degree are still very large—you should go to college if you want to earn more—but do beware of the cost.[19]

There is a big difference between graduating from college with mountains of debt and leaving college debt free. With large debts, you almost have to enter the business world immediately. Without debt, you can live abroad, work for a nonprofit, or take an internship for a year. Your options are much greater when you don't have creditors breathing down your neck. And carrying debt is that much more worrisome in the current economy where jobs are scarce.

But don't give up. There are ways to reduce the cost of college and good reasons to pursue them. First, don't be misled by the sticker price. Most students, and particularly those who are financially strapped or academically talented, don't pay the full cost of college. Almost all colleges provide financial aid for students who are admitted, which significantly reduces the amount you pay.[20]

When I was first writing this guide, I recommended that students favor public over private schools because they charged far less. After doing some research on the subject, however, I learned that with generous financial aid, a selective private school can be as cheap as, if not cheaper than, a top state university. Amherst College, a leading liberal arts college, recently introduced a pioneering program where no student is required to take out a loan if they are admitted and several other colleges have followed their lead. For most low- or moderate-income students, an elite school like Harvard will be less expensive than their home-state public university.

Unfortunately, the financial aid system at all schools has become so complicated that there are few simple rules I can recommend except one, which is to try to get the best deal you can. Consider a number of colleges and

19. Currently college graduates earn about 54 percent more than nongraduates. See Lisa Barrow and Cecilia Elena Rouse, "Does College Still Pay?" *Economists' Voice* 2, no. 4 (2005). Also see Claudin Goldin and Lawrence F. Katz, *The Race between Education and Technology* (Cambridge, MA: Harvard University Press, 2008).

20. This is not just universities being charitable. Remember that they are organized as nonprofits, which entitles them to enormous tax benefits in exchange for which they are required to provide a public service.

see which will offer you the most in terms of tuition reductions, loans, and work-study opportunities. Don't be afraid to bargain. Look widely for sources of funding—the federal government, state governments, and colleges themselves all offer financial aid. Follow the helpful advice at places like Finaid (www.finaid.org) or the College Board where you can find scholarships, loans, and calculate how much college will cost you. What is important here is to put in an effort. Don't take the first loan offered to you even if your college tells you it is the best one. Universities have behaved badly in the past, for example, colluding with banks, and it is up to you, the buyer, to beware.

TIP 7
....
Differences in the Strength of Particular Departments Are Not Usually a Good Basis for Choosing among Colleges

One might think that you should choose a college whose academic specialties best fit your interests. If you love English literature, you should go to a school that has a great English department. It is true that some universities do some subjects better than others; they have more prestigious professors in particular fields. Wisconsin has traditionally had the best sociology department in the country; Rochester is among the tops in political science. Should these differences matter to you?

In fact, there are three reasons why you should discount them. In the first place, the differences are not large. In most cases, the ranking of different departments is more or less equivalent to the ranking of the university as a whole. The two cases mentioned above are exceptions to the general rule. It is hard to think of a department at Harvard that is not among the ten best in the country; the same goes for other universities with the appropriate adjustments of rank.

The second reason is that most incoming freshmen do not really know what they want to study. Choosing a college on the basis of strength in a particular subject area can be misleading, and this is particularly true for students who haven't sampled even a portion of the academic fields offered at a university. Why choose a college based on its great English department when you haven't sampled fields like linguistics or anthropology, much less comparative literature?

Finally, these differences in quality are unlikely to trickle down to the undergraduate level and may even detract from undergraduate teaching.[21] A department that is highly rated gets its rating from the strength of its graduate program and the research productivity of its faculty. These factors have little to do with the amount of time and resources devoted to undergraduates and may even be negatively correlated with them because professors' attention is divided between undergraduates, graduate students, and their own research.

There are some exceptions to this rule, particularly for programs that have a more vocational role and are less research oriented—subjects like journalism, education, or theater. Such programs are more focused on undergraduates than the traditional academic fields, which are instead ranked by their success in research and training graduate students. And not all universities offer these vocational programs—liberal arts colleges usually will not offer any courses in journalism, engineering, or business. So do consider the existence and strength of these programs if you want to pursue them.

Another issue is specialty programs. Many colleges and universities like to boast about their unique academic programs. Their special major in the history of ideas or nanotechnology or their groundbreaking interdisciplinary programs. Don't take these claims too seriously. As I just noted, incoming freshman have very little idea about even the conventional majors, the majority of which they have never encountered before. To have already decided to move beyond this unknown to a greater unknown is jumping the gun.

To this may be added the fact that the vast majority of your professors have been trained and do their research in a specific established field that is not one of these specialty programs. When a university does decide to create a nontraditional program, they usually borrow faculty from established fields and departments. While this may lead to interesting synergies, it may also produce a no-man's land as faculty are contributing half their time to their home department and half to the new field. Established fields have also thought more deeply about their goals, methods, and even pedagogy, which usually means that they will provide a more coherent education than newer fields. This is not to dismiss these experiments; after all, the old fields were new at one point. It is only to say that these programs should probably not be decisive in your choice of a college.

21. I would add that rankings are often fleeting. It is common for a department to lose or gain a handful of talented professors and move rapidly up or down the rankings. If you are interested in the subject, see Brian Leiter's rankings of philosophy departments at www .philosophicalgourmet.com and the accompanying discussion.

CHOOSING A FOREIGN UNIVERSITY

Are you adventurous, confident, and know what you want to study? Then you might consider going abroad for your college education. Not just a study abroad program, but actually enrolling at a foreign university. Most Americans limit their college choices to the United States, but there is a whole world of universities to which Americans are free to apply from Oxford to Tokyo, from Paris to Seoul.

These universities have a number of advantages over American ones. In the first place, your education is immediately expanded to include learning a foreign culture and perhaps a foreign language. Foreign universities are often cheaper than their American counterparts (locals in fact usually pay nothing) even when they are equally prestigious. And admission mainly involves getting high enough test scores or grades rather than being president of the Spanish Club or a star athlete.

On the other hand, universities outside the United States are more specialized. Students have far less opportunity to sample different subjects and frequently have to apply to a particular department to which most of their studies are confined. Professors also tend to be more distant (and overworked). They spend less time with individual students and provide less feedback on your work. As one student put it, "There's not that kind of hand-holding [as in American universities]."* Of course, these disadvantages could be pluses for students who know where they are headed, want prestige at a reasonable price, and are curious about foreign cultures.

*Tamar Lewin, "Going Off to College for Less (Passport Required)," *New York Times*, December 1, 2008.

TIP 8

Consider the Different Varieties of General Education Programs

I have argued that most colleges and universities have similar if not identical academic programs. But one place where there are some differences is in their general education requirements, the part of the curriculum where universities try to introduce students to the broad varieties of human knowledge. Essentially, some schools have a more rigid general education curriculum—they require a lot of courses—and others give you more choices.

By far the most common model is a set of distribution requirements (along with a major field). This means that all students must take a certain number of courses in different fields of thought; the typical areas are the natural sciences, the social sciences, and the humanities, but different universities specify the distributions in different ways. This option is a middle ground—not too many requirements and not too much flexibility—which is why it has been chosen by the vast majority of colleges. It is not a perfect middle ground though. The required courses are often enough to get in the way, but not enough to constitute a coherent introduction to the subject areas they represent. (Indeed, this model often gives rise to courses like Rocks for Jocks or Physics for Poets, which typically serve no one's interest.)

For this reason you might consider one of the minority of colleges that does things differently. A number of schools like St. John's of Maryland pursue what is known as a Great Books program. That is, they require students to take a substantial core curriculum focused on the "classics" of Western (and sometimes non-Western) thought. The idea is that these great works will inspire students and provide them with all the cultural baggage that an educated person should have. On the negative side, in such a program students not only lose the ability to construct their own education, they also lose an acquaintance with the latest findings and research in many fields. Other schools take inspiration from the Great Books approach, but rather than make it a 24/7 commitment, they require a broad set of survey courses that try to cover some of the same ground as the great books while giving students more room for maneuver. Columbia's humanities requirement might fit in this compartment.[22]

On the other hand, several schools like Brown or Amherst dispense with these requirements altogether. (Brown even dispenses with majors.) This is not to say that anything goes. Most of these schools admit highly motivated students who don't shy away from unknown fields and who are encouraged to experiment through the use of pass/fail options. They also usually have a strong advising system that helps students to construct their own course of study. While it is hard to say whether these alternative programs are better

---

22. For a fascinating description of these courses by a former student who retook them thirty years later, see David Denby, *Great Books* (New York: Simon and Schuster, 1997).

or worse than the standard—research is inconclusive—they may be just what you are looking for.[23]

TIP 9
....

Don't Worry; Most Students Are Happy with Their Choice

I feel a little bad about this tip. As I said before, choosing a college is probably the first significant adult decision that most readers of this book will make. And for this reason, they put a lot of effort into making it. While I don't want to say that your choice of college is insignificant, I do want to take some of the anxiety out of it.

Ultimately, most students are happy at the school they choose. While this may be a result of researching the decision so heavily, I think it is more a consequence of the college experience itself. Colleges are tremendous socializers. Within a few weeks of showing up at a college, any college, you will learn a whole new way of living. From doing your own laundry to dealing with lots of unstructured time to learning where the parties are. You will not only learn a new way of life, but you will identify with it. You will wear sweatshirts with your college's insignia, root for your football team, and defend your college against its rivals. In short, you will feel that you belong there. And this applies to just about any college you choose. In a *New York Times* survey of recent college graduates, 54 percent viewed their undergraduate experience as excellent, 39 percent as good, and only 7 percent as fair or poor.[24]

While there is always the chance that you might have been happier or gotten a better education elsewhere, it is unlikely that you will have regrets about your choice. Most graduates identify with their alma mater until the end of their days. Why else would they continue to contribute to it? Amazingly, only 5 percent of respondents to the aforementioned poll said that they would go to a different school if they had it to do over again, and only 4 percent said that they made the wrong choice. Perhaps even more tell-

---

23. One study found that "the varieties of general education programs currently used in American higher education do not seem to make much difference in any aspect of the student's cognitive or affective development." See Alexander W. Astin, *What Matters in Education: Four Critical Years Revisited* (San Francisco: Jossey-Bass, 1993), p. 334.

24. *New York Times* Alumni Poll, June 15–23, 2007.

ing are the small numbers of transfers each year. The same poll found that 73 percent of students complete their education at only one school and 12 percent move from a two-year to a four-year college, while only 13 percent moved from one four-year college to another. Students could easily be moving from one university to the next, but they tend not to. If they leave, it is usually because they are not ready for or interested in the college experience, not because they went to the wrong place.

And as I have argued, the American college experience is fairly homogeneous—the whole gamut of courses and majors, not to mention student bodies, dorms, and parties, are pretty much the same at every university. All the groups laid out in the film *The Breakfast Club* are represented just about anywhere—the brain, the athlete, the basket case, the princess, and the criminal. This is why any American college graduate can watch a film like *Animal House* and immediately see that it represents the (not a) college experience. It is no coincidence that John "Bluto" Blutarsky wears a t-shirt bearing the single word "College." Perhaps the college experience should be more diverse and there should be more options. In fact it is not and there are not, so don't make the choice too hard for yourself.

Choosing Classes

Every semester, students confront the dilemma of what classes to take. Many look harried and disappointed during registration week and the first week of classes. The cause of their disappointment is not that all the good courses are filled up—even if students think they are—but that they wear blinders in making their choices. Rather than consider the full range of courses at the university, their eyes narrow to a limited number of choices that they believe are the only ones that fit their interests and academic plans. Taking off these blinders will reveal an incredible number of fascinating courses at every university, many of which have plenty of open seats.

The first mistake that students make is in sticking to their comfort zone. They only take classes they think they will like and do well in. If presented with a radically new or different option, they will usually take a pass. A real education, however, will confront them with genuinely new ideas. And in retrospect students agree with this. When a recent survey asked graduates what they would do differently if they had to repeat their university experience, the most popular answer at three selective schools was to take more courses, to take more diverse courses, and to do more research.[1] The tips here are intended to open students' eyes to this variety as well as to get them into courses that will challenge their preconceptions.

The second mistake is a lack of diligence in seeking out the best professors. Classes differ not just in subject matter, but in the quality of the instructor. There are great teachers and terrible ones. This is partially the nature of the beast—teaching is more an art than a science—but it also reflects the incentives at universities. Professors are not rewarded for teaching

---

1.Twelve to 14 percent of students chose this option, and 8–10 percent said that not doing this was their biggest regret. See *New York Times* Alumni Poll, June 15 –23, 2007.

well. Those who do teach well and devote themselves to undergraduates are therefore doing it from the kindness of their own hearts.

Ultimately, the professor makes or breaks the class. As students your challenge is simply to identify as many great professors as possible. You need to find those souls who have a natural talent for teaching and who care about students. I would add that great teaching is not a single thing. You may disagree with your friends on which professors are the best. Some may prefer charismatic, outspoken ones; others more restrained personalities; some like formality and distinguished professors; others informality and youthful enthusiasm. You don't have to follow the crowd to those considered the best. You have plenty of chances to decide for yourself which professors and teaching styles suit you. The tips to follow will help you in identifying these professors.

TIP 10

Consider Visiting Multiple Classes during the First Week of the Semester

Universities require you to register for classes before the semester begins, and many classes do fill up before your registration time rolls around. But most universities have liberal rules about changing classes during the first week or two of the new semester. And rarely do all worthwhile courses fill up even at the end of the course change period.

You should view these rules as a loophole that allows you to make better choices. What I would recommend is the following. During the first week of classes, go to between five and ten different classes. Try a different class at every time slot. (Of course, beware of classes that require you to attend the first session.) While this may keep you running around for that week, it won't be too bad because professors generally do not teach very intensively at the start of the term precisely because students are switching in and out of classes. And it will yield a number of dividends.

Sampling multiple classes will provide you an early impression of which courses are good and which are not. As the next tip shows, most people can make good evaluations of classes relatively quickly. Just seeing the professor in action once is usually enough. You will also be able to look at the syllabus and see what sort of material is covered and in what way. You can get a rough idea of a professor's devotion to teaching by the kind of assignments in their syllabus. Professors who are committed to their students tend to give more feedback and are less likely to assign just a midterm and final or a single final paper. If you want to improve your efficiency, a lot of this groundwork can be conducted before the semester starts. Many professors post their syllabi online, and you can browse a course's required texts in the bookstore even before the term starts.

This approach will also provide you with a mini-introduction to many different fields. Even in the course of one or two lectures, you will see what different subjects have to offer. And the syllabi will provide you with a nice reading list if you ever get interested in the topic of classes you don't end up taking. (I am an inveterate collector of syllabi for this very reason.)

Obviously you won't be able to sign up for every good class you attend, but you will for some, and you will also develop a stock of courses that you wish to take in the future. Because certain material needs to be covered for each new crop of students, the same courses are offered year after year. (The Harvard philosophy professor Robert Nozick reputedly never taught the same class twice, but he is the exception.) Even if you can't take a course during one semester, you will likely get another opportunity later. And as important as finding the right subject matter is finding the right professor. While you may not get the exact same course a second time, you will surely be able to catch the same professor again and this is just as good.

TIP 11

Usually Trust Your First Impressions

In his best-selling book *Blink*, the *New Yorker* journalist Malcolm Gladwell relates how people can make surprisingly accurate judgments literally in the blink of an eye.[2] The subconscious mind is good at sizing up situations even before the conscious mind starts thinking about them. This insight can be useful in choosing courses. If you love (or hate) your professor on first sight, your opinion is likely not going to change later.

Research on student evaluations of professors backs this up. In one experiment students were shown a silent thirty-second video clip of a professor teaching and were then asked to evaluate the quality of his teaching.[3]

2. Malcolm Gladwell, *Blink: The Power of Thinking without Thinking* (New York: Little, Brown, and Company, 2005). Though see Richard Posner, "Blinkered," *New Republic*, January 24, 2005, for the limits of his argument.

3. Nalini Ambady and Robert Rosenthal, "Half a Minute: Predicting Teacher Evaluations from Thin Slices of Nonverbal Behavior and Physical Attractiveness," *Journal of Personality and Social Psychology* 64, no. 3 (1993): 431–41.

Amazingly, their evaluations based on this short, silent clip were almost identical to those of students who had experienced the professor's teaching for the entire semester, presumably with sound. First impressions in short seem to be lasting impressions.

One first impression that I sometimes consider is whether a professor uses innovative teaching methods—that is, something besides the standard lecture or discussion format. The reason is not that these innovations are necessarily better, but that they are a sign that the professor has actually thought about teaching and cares enough to work on it. And if they care that much, they will be helpful to you in other ways too.

I would add one caveat to this advice. Much of an education is challenging your own biases. When you first encounter a professor who really and genuinely challenges those preconceptions, you may react negatively. But that is precisely the class you need to be in to examine your prejudices and find your way to truth. If you are a libertarian, you need to be in sociology classes. If you are socialist, you need to be in economics classes. In these cases, first impressions can be misleading.

PRIORITIES IN CHOOSING CLASSES

I can't say for certain how my students go about choosing their classes, but my experience suggests that they follow certain rules. Most seem to start by trying to satisfy requirements. These might be distributional requirements, required courses for their major, or required classes for graduate school. They then think about balance—they want to make sure they don't have too many hard classes or writing classes or math classes—and try to make sure that they don't have too many classes early in the morning or on Fridays. Having limited themselves in these ways— and to certain subjects they know well—they then start thinking about what subjects look interesting and who the best professors are.

I would suggest reversing these priorities (see the table below). I would begin by trying to identify the best professors at your college. I have suggested some ways of doing so in this chapter. Most of your best educational experiences will come from great professors. Your first priority should be finding them. I would then suggest looking at new subjects, subjects that will develop your skills in thinking or writing, and subjects that will challenge your preconceptions. Once you have assembled these classes, you are almost guaranteed a great semester.

Only then would I turn to balance and requirements. While an unbalanced schedule might overwhelm you, if all the courses you are taking are stimulating, then you probably won't mind doing the extra work. And while I don't suggest that you ignore requirements—I do want you to graduate—you should start by trying to get the best education you can and think about requirements only once you have found your way around and can choose requirements that fit your needs. (I would add that there are sometimes ways around requirements; if you make a compelling case to the relevant administrator, you can often substitute other classes for the ones you were supposed to take.)

Priorities in Choosing Classes

Students' Priorities	*My Suggested Priorities*
1. Requirements	1. Great Professors
2. Balance	2. New Subjects
3. Interesting Subjects	3. Balance
4. Good Professors	4. Requirements

TIP 12

....

Go for Variety, Especially Early On

In most countries outside of the United States, students apply not to a university but to a particular department, say chemistry or history, and then study more or less exclusively in that department. American universities are different. Their presumption is that students enter college without knowing what they want to study. Indeed, high school students are not introduced to most of the subjects that they can study in college. How many high schools offer classes in African American studies, anthropology, art history, or astronomy, to cover only the A's? In fact, even four years is not enough time to sample every department at a university—a large one may have a hundred departments, a smaller one thirty—much less the different idea streams in each.

In order to find out what you enjoy doing and what you do well, you thus need to sample a large variety of courses. Every discipline has a unique perspective on the world—a set of questions it asks and ways of addressing them. Only by immersing yourself in a number of these perspectives can you figure which ways suit you the best. As a freshman and sophomore, you should take at least one course each semester that is a complete and total flyer—a subject you know little about but which sounds intriguing. Most will not stick, but one or two may. As a side effect of this experimentation, you will also understand the world much better. The more ways of knowing that you learn, the better equipped you are to make sense of the diverse situations you will encounter throughout your life.

TIP 13
....

At Least Once a Year Pick a Class That Doesn't Seem to Fit Your Interests

Challenging your biases is hard. It hurts to have your worldview called into question. Yet, a real education requires you to do exactly this. An education tries to make us see the world as it really is. But without training, the human mind sees the world only through a glass darkly. We view politics through our partisan preferences, ethics through our religious upbringing, and so on. Most of these prejudices are so ingrained that we don't even notice them. For that reason they are even more insidious and require a full frontal challenge.

Every year search the course catalog for a course that you know you will hate or disagree with. For some it will be "Introduction to Women's Studies," for others "Biological Differences between the Sexes." It may be "Conservative Political Thought" or "Marx and His Followers." The important thing is that you are going to disagree with the basic premises of the course.

The reason for choosing a course like this is that people have a strong tendency to confirm their own prejudices and insulate themselves from alternative views. Several years ago I heard a pollster from Gallup discussing the popularity ratings of politicians. An irate caller to the program claimed that their surveys were systematically biased. "How," she asked, "could George W. Bush have approval ratings of 70%?" (This was back in 2002.) She didn't know one person who approved of his performance. The pollster patiently explained that this was in fact the purpose of polls. People choose their acquaintances so carefully that they are rarely exposed to opposing viewpoints. Only a truly random sample of the population can tell you what the country as a whole is thinking. Indeed, he had received the same complaints a few years earlier when Bill Clinton had equally high approval ratings. Back then people were calling in to say that they didn't know one person who approved of Clinton.

The same applies to choosing classes. Left to their own devices, most students will choose classes that confirm their prejudices and strengths without even knowing that they are doing this. What is needed is some mechanism to force them to confront alternatives. That is the justification for this tip. It is the equivalent of the pollster's use of random selection. At least once in a while, you should select a course that you would not have selected on your own. Even if you hate it in the end, you will have learned more than by taking one more course that intentionally or not confirms your current beliefs.

TIP 14
....

Take Classes with Heavy Writing Requirements

While college is not primarily a place to learn practical skills, there is at least one skill that you need to pick up as a part of your education. That is the skill to write quickly and well. There is hardly a job for college graduates that does not require them to write clear and intelligible prose on a daily basis. If you learn nothing else in college, make sure that you can produce a coherent eight-hundred-word argument in less than an hour.

This applies across the curriculum. Consider the following comments of the owner of a computer programming firm, a sector where one would think that writing matters little if at all:

> Would Linux have succeeded if Linus Torvalds hadn't evangelized it? As brilliant a hacker as he is, it was Linus's ability to convey his ideas in written English via email and mailing lists that made Linux attract a worldwide brigade of volunteers. . . .
>
> Even on the small scale, when you look at any programming organization, the programmers with the most power and influence are the ones who can write and speak in English clearly, convincingly, and comfortably. . . .
>
> The difference between a tolerable programmer and a great programmer is not how many programming languages they know, and it's not whether they prefer Python or Java. It's whether they can communicate their ideas. By persuading other people, they get leverage.[4]

These remarks apply to an even greater extent in fields where writing is more common.

While all colleges profess a commitment to developing the writing skills

4. See Joel Spolsky, "Advice for Computer Science College Students," www.joelonsoftware .com.

of their students, few do it as well as they should.[5] Writing should be a constant part of every student's education, but faculty shrink from teaching it. Most professors are trained in a particular subject, not in the art of composition. Teaching writing is also hard. It requires professors to devote a lot of effort to each piece of writing they receive—often very poor ones. This is a large time commitment for which professors receive little or no reward.

As a result, teaching composition is outsourced—to the English department and then to graduate students or part-timers.[6] But this is far from ideal. While scholars of English literature may be experts on style, just about all professors make their living by writing and are capable of teaching students the principles of good writing. Best then would be to write across the curriculum—to have practice writing essays about political science, philosophy, history, and even economics, biology, and physics. This has the added advantage of giving students the opportunity to write about issues that interest them, which makes the training more effective. But few colleges have writing-intensive courses in multiple subjects.

What do good writing classes look like? The way to develop writing skills is the same way you get to Carnegie Hall—practice, practice, practice. Writing a short essay or two every week or better every day is best. (Extensive reading is of course vital too.) But most classes do not require you to write very much. Most universities have an introductory set of writing-intensive seminars—often only one course—but they stop there. Better would be more of them. When Richard Light interviewed graduating seniors he found that many would have preferred writing seminars to be given in junior and senior year when they were ready for them and desired them.[7] As freshmen, they didn't realize the importance of writing and had too little time to devote to it. You would be well advised to seek out as many classes labeled "writing intensive" as you can find.

Nearly as important as quantity is feedback. You need to hand in the assignment, get critical comments, and incorporate these comments into future assignments or even revisions of the same piece. Don't choose courses

---

5. According to one scholar, "Responsible administration of a university writing program is a test of the institution's integrity, a test few institutions can pass at the minimum competency level." See Edward M. White, *Developing Successful College Writing Programs* (San Francisco: Jossey-Bass, 1989), p. 164

6. See Louis Menand, "The Ph.D. Problem," *Harvard Magazine*, November–December 2009.

7. Richard J. Light, *Making the Most of College: Students Speak Their Minds* (Cambridge, MA: Harvard University Press, 2001), pp. 54–62.

with a single twenty-page final paper—or at least don't choose them to improve your writing—choose ones with short weekly or biweekly papers. The ideal might be what is common in graduate school where students are required to write two-to-three-page reactions to the week's readings each and every week. Such a model seems to pay off for graduate students who use it to become experts in their field in scarcely more than a year.

The beauty of such intensive writing is not only that it forces you to practice, but it also requires professors to focus their attention on you specifically. They have to engage your efforts every week in a personal way. This is the reason why such courses are not as common as they should be—they take up a lot of faculty energy. But it is exactly for this reason that you should seek them out. Indeed, the amount of writing required in a course is one measure of a professor's devotion to her students. If a professor requires a lot of writing, this means that she has committed herself to spending a lot of time on the class because she is going to have to grade all of these essays and get into the heads of all the students in the class.

Finally, all of this writing has benefits for learning more generally. Writing intensively forces you to come to terms with the course material, which is why courses with a lot of writing have higher levels of student engagement.[8] And there is evidence that putting material into narrative form—in short, writing about it—is one of the best ways for the brain to absorb new ideas.[9] In short, you are learning not just how to write better, but how to think better.

TIP 15

Take as Many Small Seminars and as Few Large Lecture Courses as Possible

If you want to get your money's worth at college, minimize the number of large lecture courses you take (or audit them as Tip 26 suggests). This is the place where universities skimp and save. Lectures allow them to teach a lot of students with very few teachers. The upshot is obvious. In a class of one student, you get 100 percent of the professor's attention. In a class of

8. Richard Light has found that courses with frequent writing assignments are also viewed as more interesting and challenging than other courses. See ibid., p. 55.

9. See Robert H. Frank, *The Economic Naturalist: In Search of Explanations for Everyday Enigmas* (New York: Basic Books, 2007). Frank has students in his introductory economics course write short essays explaining an unusual economic phenomenon.

ten, you get on average 10 percent. What then do you get in a class of one hundred? One percent is probably a high estimate as a professor's eyes blur at the mass of students. You cannot expect individualized attention and personal feedback in these classes.

This is not to say that lecture classes are all bad. Often you will find brilliant and charismatic professors who seem to give you your money's worth and even find ways of engaging with students; though nearly as often you will encounter the opposite.

But a great performance is just about all you will get.[10] Otherwise, most if not all of your contact is with a TA who makes sure you do the assignments, grades your papers, and perhaps leads a discussion section. Yes, some TAs are smart and devoted, but is this what you are paying tuition for? Lectures also tend to emphasize passive learning (the professor talks, the student takes notes) over active learning (where students engage with problems themselves).[11] One of the main findings of educational research is that active learning leads to better outcomes than passive learning.[12]

Not only are you getting less out of lectures, but there is a cheap substitute that is often of higher quality than most of the classes you are taking. Just buy CDs or DVDs of great lectures from places like the Learning Company (www.thegreatcourses.com) or access free videos of lectures from a new Youtube page (www.youtube.com/edu).[13] There is a high probability

10. The economist Brad Delong asks why the lecture emerged if it is not the best way to learn. He argues that in medieval times when the university arose, books were too expensive for students to own (this was before the printing press). Thus, professors had to read them out loud (lecture is from the Latin lector or reader) while students frantically scribbled down their contents. See Brad DeLong, "Why Are We Here? (In a Big Lecture, That Is)," delong.typepad.com.

11. One study found that 73–83 percent of professors simply lecture passively to their students. See Derek Bok, *Our Underachieving Colleges: A Candid Look at How Much Students Learn and Why They Should Be Learning More* (Princeton, NJ: Princeton University Press, 2006), p. 120.

12. Greg Light, Roy Cox, and Susanna Calkins, *Learning and Teaching in Higher Education: The Reflective Professional*, 2nd ed. (Los Angeles: Sage Publications, 2009).

13. As Steven Pearlstein puts it, "Every year . . . there are thousands of college professors who twice or three times a week offer what is largely the same basic lecture course in a subject like molecular biology or Shakespeare comedies. A few of these professors offer the kind of brilliant lectures that fill auditoriums and provide the kind of educational experience that students remember all their lives. Many of the rest offer something that ranges from mediocre to awful. . . . Why don't we identify these extraordinary lecturers, put their lectures on CDs, and sell them to universities that could supplement them with faculty-led tutorials

that these lectures are going to be better than the ones offered at your university. It may be pushing the point to say these videos are equivalent to lecture courses at your college—you probably lose something without the live performance and the pressure to do the assignments—but they do come quite close. If you feel that you need the theatrical experience, then just sit in on the classes of the best lecturers at your university without signing up for them (see Tip 26).

By contrast, consider what you are getting out of a small seminar course. In the first place, the professor will know you—your face, your name, your ideas, your writing. And he or she will be forced to react to your thoughts whether in class or on your assignments. My undergraduate college had as its image of the ideal education, "The Log." According to legend, President James A. Garfield said of one of his former professors that "the ideal college is Mark Hopkins on one end of a log and the student on the other." This image encapsulates the way that most people conceive an education. And seminars are the closet approximation you will find at American universities. (British universities offer tutorials where you actually get this one-on-one encounter.)

Seminars will also force you to fully engage with the course material. Because you are in the spotlight during every class and forced to put forward your own ideas, you will have to actively digest your assignments. Not only will you be under pressure to do the reading—something that slips by the wayside in large lecture courses—but you will have to think about it and come up with insights and criticisms to share in class. Seminars are as much a disciplining force—forcing you to stay alert—as a place where you receive personalized attention.[14]

And research backs up this advice. When Richard Light interviewed graduating seniors, he found that the number of small classes taken correlated highly with satisfaction and even with grades.[15] Students who took more seminar-style classes were more satisfied *and* received higher grades!

This advice does not apply across the board. There are certain shy souls

---

or discussions?" The religion professor Mark Taylor tried to put such a scheme in place at Williams College, but it was voted down by the faculty. See Steven Pearlstein, "The Lesson Colleges Need to Learn," *Washington Post*, December 17, 2003.

14. The discipline applies to professors as well. They have to work harder to prepare for a seminar than a lecture.

15. Light, *Making the Most of College*, pp. 46–50. I suspect that it is easier for a professor to give a low grade to a student they have never met than to one they know well.

(like myself) who are too timid to engage in seminars and thus do not get the most out of them. Four seminars each quarter may also put a strain on your time. You may need to "relax" at a lecture course to keep up your steam (that is what these courses often are—relaxation). For seminars to pay off, you have to invest in them—engaging the assignments and your fellow students. Without this investment they might be worth less than lectures. But with it, they will give you far more. An additional bonus of these classes is that you will get to know your professor personally, a benefit I will describe in chapter 6.

WHAT DOES A GOOD LECTURE LOOK LIKE?

It is sometimes hard to tell if a lecturer is doing a good job or not. Students do not always know whether they are truly learning from a lecture or simply being entertained. Educational research, however, has started to understand the styles of teaching that lead to better learning.* Students appear to learn best when lecturers do the following things:

1. *Good lecturers allow students the opportunity to participate.* Even in large lecture classes—over one hundred students—good lecturers find ways to get students involved whether by letting them voice their opinions, conducting spot polls or quizzes, or initiating small group discussions. If there is little role for students to play in your classroom—the professor spends the whole period talking—you may be better off trying another class.

2. *Good lecturers base their lectures around problems.* A good lecture almost always begins with a question, problem, or puzzle and shows students its significance. A good lecture then provides students an opportunity to grapple with the problem themselves. Only sometimes do professors provide an answer to the problem. But what a good lecture always does is leave students with a new problem to ponder at the end of class. This sort of problem-based lecturing is more likely to promote engagement and learning than other approaches.

3. *Good lecturers show students the personal relevance of the material.* Students tend not to learn as well when the material only seems

*See Ken Bain, *What the Best College Teachers Do* (Cambridge, MA: Harvard University Press, 2004)

relevant to success in the course. Good lecturers show how the material has wider relevance to their lives and careers. If your teacher has not shown you the relevance of the course, then consider another professor.

4. *Good lecturers don't overload students with information.* Most students cannot hold their attention on a lecture beyond about fifteen minutes. Good lecturers will find ways to present information in digestible chunks and vary the mode of presentation frequently, using video, audio, or hands-on activities. If your professor goes on for much longer than this in a single format—for example, simply talking—then you might not be learning as much as you could.

TIP 16

Take Mostly Upper-Division Courses

When Harvard experimented with a curriculum devoid of requirements early in the twentieth century, most students ended up only taking introductory courses. Even today many students tend to stick with lower-division courses unless they know the subject well. By all means start your academic career with lower-level courses—in the standard nomenclature 100- or 200-level classes—but it is mistake to stick with them for a number of reasons.[16]

In the first place, lower-division courses are less challenging than upper-division ones. They treat subjects superficially and are designed for the masses, the lowest common denominator student. And because they usually have large enrollments, the mode of instruction is typically the passive transmission of knowledge: a professor lectures and students take notes. To top it off, most professors dislike teaching these classes because they have to stray outside of their specialties to cover the material. Yes, you will get a panoramic survey of a field from these courses that helps to broaden your knowledge, but your mind will probably not be tested.

In upper-division courses, by contrast, professors will start pushing you. They will give you more complex exercises and more room to engage with

16. Upper-division courses are typically numbered in the 300s or 400s while graduate courses would be in the 500s; however, many different course numbering systems exist. One university recently contemplated renumbering their courses because the low numbers supposedly made their courses look too easy to outsiders. See Michael Munger, "Great Moments in Faculty Meetings," mungowitzend.blogspot.com.

problems. These classes are also smaller and thus provide you with more personal contact with the instructor and more individualized feedback on your assignments. Instructors are more engaged too because the material is closer to their areas of expertise. Though the subject may be narrower, this is not such a worry because you are unlikely to remember the material in any case. What you are learning are thinking skills and upper-division classes will give you these more than lower-division ones.

TIP 17

....

Focus More on Methods Than Topics

Most departments offer some courses that tell you how their field operates—the techniques it uses to understand the world—and others that tell you what scholars have found using those techniques. The first type is referred to as a methods course and the second as a topics course. The first might be titled "Methods of Political Inquiry" or "Statistics for Political Science," while the second might be called "Elections and Voting" or "The Politics of Africa." The line is not hard and fast. Methods are almost always presented in the context of an actual topic and courses on a specific topic necessarily introduce a variety of methods. The difference is more one of emphasis and design.

My advice is to take as many methods courses as you can. It is these courses that teach ways of thinking and understanding that will stick with you. The facts and theories that you learn in topics courses will be quickly forgotten no matter how interesting they seem at the time. While you might feel like an expert in African politics at the end of a semester, a few months later you will have only a hazy sense of who succeeded Mobuto Sese Seko and why apartheid fell. You will also forget some of what you learned in methods courses, but since these courses will typically teach you one big thing, they are more memorable. The big thing is how to identify and approach a problem. Once you have learned this one thing—and these courses typically hammer it in—it is likely to stick with you. You will come to view every problem you encounter in its light.

The difference is neatly summed up in the well-known proverb "Give a man a fish and he'll eat for a day, teach him how to fish and he'll eat forever." Methods courses teach you how to fish, how to approach a problem like a sociologist or art historian or biologist. While it would be going too far to say that topics courses only give you a fish—most professors put methods into every course—the fishing skills they teach are less distilled and intense and so may pass you by. Surveys of graduating seniors confirm that learning how to think like a member of a discipline—which is what methods course do—leads students to study a subject in more depth.[17]

I would add that you should sample methods courses from around the curriculum—from the humanities, social sciences, and natural sciences.[18] Most majors have at least one required course in methods, but don't limit yourself to the methods of your major. Each field approaches the world in a different way (and sometimes multiple ways), and it behooves you to learn the essence of each perspective. While a topics course in a field will pique your interest, a methods course will give you something to take away permanently.

TIP 18

Seek Out Classes That Provide You with Continuous Feedback and Take the Feedback Seriously

If you want to learn from your classes, you need to complete your assignments and then get feedback about what you did poorly and what you did well. Without these pointers it is nearly impossible to improve your performance. How do you know where you made mistakes (much less how to fix them) if no one tells you?

One of the ways you can do this is by taking classes from professors who require a lot of assignments and return them with detailed comments. (This is one more advantage of writing intensive courses—see Tip 14.) A class with a single exam or final paper usually does not provide you with much insight into what you are doing poorly and how to improve. In fact, most of my students rarely bother to pick up their final exams and papers even after I tell them that they will be available in my office for several weeks into the following semester. Needless to say, you should always pick them up.

It is then incumbent upon you to take this feedback seriously. Don't focus on the bottom line grade. Look at the professor's actual comments on your

---

17. Light, *Making the Most of College*, pp. 117–19.

18. Actually, pretty much all courses in the natural sciences are methods courses. After all, labs are teaching you the actual methods of science.

work and try to learn from them. Figure out where you went wrong and how to do things differently next time. If it is not clear where you screwed up, seek out the professor at his office hours and ask what you should be doing differently. Even if you did well, try to find out where you can improve. Without getting feedback and taking it seriously, you are only getting half of an education.

TIP 19
....

Know the Status of Your Professors

Professors come in a variety of shapes and sizes. Some of the main distinctions are tenured versus untenured, tenure-track versus nontenure-track, and full-time versus part-time. Which of these types is going to give you the best education? The answer is not obvious. All of them may be great or terrible teachers, and it is their teaching abilities that usually matter the most. But these differences of status and rank can inform your course choices.

The most prestigious species of the professor genus is the full-time tenured professor. They can be recognized on their department Web site by the full professor or associate professor title or by their tweed jacket with elbow patches (just joking). That they are tenured means that they have produced scholarship that is important and original in the opinion of their peers. More practically, it means that they cannot be fired (or only for serious transgressions of university rules, not general incompetence).

While these are the most prestigious birds in the zoo, does that mean they will give you the best education? Possibly. On the positive side, you have some assurance that they really know their field and are (or once were) active contributors to it. And if you are a sucker for the confident, distinguished type, they epitomize it. On the negative side, they may be such active contributors to their field that they have little time for lowly undergraduates. And because they have tenure, no one can force them to do a better job. Indeed, insiders refer to a special subtype of this species as deadwood, meaning that because they have tenure and cannot be fired, they no longer devote energy to either scholarship or teaching.

The next category down on the totem pole is tenure-track full-time faculty. You can recognize them by the assistant professor title. They have been hired recently, usually fresh out of graduate school, and are given six years or so to prove—mostly through research—that they are worthy of tenure.[19] Like law firms and the military, universities typically have an up or out rule so that either you get tenure and stay or don't get it and seek work elsewhere (almost always at a less prestigious school).

Because these faculty are more or less single-mindedly focused on tenure, they spend most of their free hours trying to produce serious research.[20] Because they are lower on the totem pole than senior faculty (senior means tenured, junior untenured), they often have to do a considerable amount of teaching. They are also likely teaching for the first time—as graduate students they mostly served as TAs—and developing their own courses from scratch.

While this may sound like an inauspicious combination for producing great teaching, such faculty do have advantages. They are fresh to the field and still have a large degree of enthusiasm that has often been worn away in older faculty. The content of their courses is closer to the state-of-the-art in knowledge, and they are more likely to come up with interesting, new courses. Because they are younger, you may be better able to relate with them on a personal level. You might also see them around the department more because they have fewer outside responsibilities.

Although tenure for assistant professors is mostly connected with research productivity, some colleges and universities do consider the quality of their teaching. The implicit standard, however, is usually a negative one— universities do not want to tenure teachers who inspire complaints—but they are relatively indifferent toward mediocre teachers. (Liberal arts colleges have higher standards here.) As a result, untenured faculty have some incentives to teach better, but not particularly strong ones.

These two groups used to form the heart of most colleges and universities, but there is a group of "others"—known generically as adjuncts— who carry an increasingly large share of the teaching load (our profession's version of outsourcing). They come in various forms. There are advanced graduate students who are allowed to teach their own classes. There are full-time lecturers who are typically hired for their teaching skills, but do not

19. This is referred to as their probationary period, and for some it feels like being on probation.

20. A movie called *Tenure* recently premiered at the Sundance Film Festival, but was a flop. The reason may be the lack of excitement in trying to get tenure. As one professor put it, "since my ongoing pursuit of tenure typically involves me sitting in front of my laptop until 1 a.m., I don't know how interesting that would be to watch." See Scott Jaschik, "Tenure, the Movie," *Inside Higher Ed*, March 18, 2008.

have tenure, are not expected to produce research, and are usually poorly paid. There are various visitors—whether postdoctoral fellows, foreign academics visiting America, or individuals with relevant real-world experience. And there are part-timers who are hired to teach a course or two that the department cannot cover without outside help. This other category typically goes under titles like lecturer, adjunct professor, or visiting assistant professor (sometimes tenure-track faculty who have not finished their dissertation use these titles, but only temporarily).

How should you judge these others? It is difficult to make any obvious recommendations. Permanent lecturers are often the best teachers in the department because that is the basis of their appointment and they do not have other commitments like research. They can devote all of their time to undergraduates. They do, however, lack the prestige of their tenured or tenure-track colleagues and usually are not as well versed in the latest developments in the field; they may be teaching material whose sell-by date is long expired.

Graduate students are under large pressures to finish their dissertation and get a job, so their attention may not be completely focused on teaching; they of course lack experience as well. They are, however, the most open to forming personal bonds with students because they are students themselves. The rest of this category is a mixed bag. Visitors can be very good or very bad. They may try to impress in order to get a full-time position, or they may view their visiting year as a vacation. What you should keep in mind about all of these part-timers is that they may not be around later if you need a letter of recommendation.

Having said all of this, I would note that recent research has shown that these distinctions do not seem to have systematic effects. As one study put it, "Whether an instructor teaches full-time or part-time, does research, has tenure, or is highly paid has no influence on a college student's grade, likelihood of dropping a course, or taking more subsequent courses in the same subject."[21] What does seem to affect these outcomes is rather the quality of a professor as evaluated by students. It is to these evaluations that I turn now.

21. Florian Hoffman and Philip Oreopoulos, "Professor Qualities and Student Achievement," NBER Working Paper 12596, October 2006. Another recent paper found that "adjunct and graduate assistant instructors generally reduce subsequent interest in a subject relative to full-time faculty members, but the effects are small and differ by discipline. Adjuncts and graduate assistants negatively affect students in the humanities while positively affecting students in some of the technical and professional fields." See also Eric Bettinger and Bridget

TIP 20

....

Learn to Be a Critical Reader of Student Evaluations of Faculty

Most universities have students fill out an evaluation of every course they take. The results are often (and definitely should be) made publicly available and can be a good guide to the best classes. In fact, a large number of studies have shown some of the benefits of these evaluations.[22] In the first place, they are reliable; students tend to agree with each other on which classes are good and even ten years later still rate the same classes highly.[23] They also appear to be correlated with performance; students perform better in classes they rate highly. In one study, two professors taught the same class and gave identical exams; students taught by the professor with higher evaluations performed better on the exam. For these reasons you should take these evaluations seriously.

On the other hand, there are a number of well-known biases in student evaluations. As you might expect, professors who give out higher grades get higher evaluations. In one survey, 70 percent of students admitted that their evaluation was influenced by their expected final grade. Evaluations are also influenced by extraneous factors like the teacher's looks and their use of acting techniques. In one study—called the Dr. Fox study—students gave high marks to a professional actor who was instructed to give a contradictory and nonsubstantive talk.[24] And in another a professor improved his evaluations considerably simply by incorporating gestures into his lectures. In short, the correlation between evaluations and education is less than perfect.

I would add that evaluations represent the opinions of the average student. Average students may be more influenced by the external charms of the class—its entertainment value—than by its substance. Average students may be bored by lectures that are too subtle and complicated or that re-

---

Terry Long, "Do College Instructors Matter? The Effects of Adjuncts and Graduate Assistants on Students' Interests and Success," NBER Working Paper 10370, March 2004.

22. This section follows Michael Huemer, "Student Evaluations: A Critical Review," home.sprynet.com/~owl1/sef.htm.

23. Interestingly, when faculty observe each other, they tend not to agree on their evaluations.

24. This study has been criticized for asking misleading questions, and later replications have yielded weaker results. See Ken Bain, *What the Best College Teachers Do* (Cambridge, MA: Harvard University Press, 2004), pp. 12–13.

quire a lot of previous knowledge. I would guess that many of the very best scholars are not among the highest rated teachers though they may have the most to offer. To get the most out of college, it is often worth seeking out these professors even if their evaluations are not the best. What I would concentrate on is students' evaluations of how much a professor cares about students and devotes attention to them and the class; it is hard to get much out of a professor who feels disdain or indifference toward students.

I would caution students, however, about taking independent Web sites like www.RateMyProfessors.com too seriously. Unlike university-sponsored evaluations that try to capture the opinions of all students who have taken a course, these sites rely on voluntary contributions and are therefore more likely to pick up those with a special axe to grind. A sense of what these sites collect can be found in one journalist's description,

> All across this great collegiate land, students want pretty much the same things. Don't play favorites, yet don't deny students extra credit or a second chance on a paper or test. Don't "get sidetracked by boring crap." Don't refer to yourself in the third person. Don't ever call on students. Don't be "mean," "hateful," or "ambiguous." Don't take attendance. Don't be "high on Viagra and full of yourself." Don't be "distractingly spastic." Very important: Don't talk about stuff in class and then put other stuff on the test. Most important: Don't give low grades. Do show slides. Do offer easy assignments. Do crack jokes and "provide a fun teaching atmosphere." Do show up at your office hours. Do give A's on all group projects. Do walk your dog around campus. Do resemble a celebrity of some sort. Finally, try your best to be "awesome."[25]

Finally, I would note that professors tend to be suspicious of student evaluations. Most believe they are only weakly correlated with learning. While research does not back this up, one can forgive them for getting this impression from the written comments they receive. Few comments are related to the substance of the course and many concern irrelevant issues like the professor's appearance or wardrobe. Most of us have our own set of favorite comments that seem to come from an alien planet. Here is how the sociologist Kieran Healy glosses a recent set of evaluations (even as he recognizes the value of the exercise):

> Arizona asks for freeform comments on two questions: What did you especially like about this course? And, What suggestions would you make to

---

25. Michael Agger, "The Hottest Professor on Campus: What Happens When Students Rate Their Teachers Online," *Slate*, November 17, 2005.

improve this course? Past highlights . . . include, "No more tucked-in shirts without a belt" and "This course would be better if it wasn't required." As expected, the comments from [last semester] cover a range. Some of the better ones:

Edifying: "Instructor knows his shit." "Actually interesting!"

Possibly misguided: "[Please provide] More suggestions for my own life with regard to my business decisions."

Praise or not? "Professor was ironic." "[I liked] the ability of the instructor to make a not so interesting subject somewhat interesting." "The teacher had his own way of teaching."

Campus identity politics scandal narrowly avoided: "Don't insult the Scottish. We may not have preserved the written word during the Dark Ages but we are a proud people none the less."[26]

The point is that if you want to improve the quality of undergraduate teaching, try to give your professors serious and constructive advice on these surveys. They are not your opportunity to get revenge, but to help the professor improve his or her teaching as he or she has presumably been helping you. (See text box "How to Improve Your Professors.")

TIP 21

Ask Professors You Know What Courses They Would Recommend

While student evaluations give you a sense of what other students think about classes, professors may also have a good idea of which ones are worth taking. It can thus be useful to ask your current or favorite professors which classes they would recommend. While they haven't taken classes in their own department, they often have a good sense of what their colleagues are like. They know who the acknowledged experts are and who is just faking it. They know who devotes time and energy to undergraduate teaching and who does not. They know who has won teaching awards and who has not. And they know each other's personalities, often too well.

As a result, they are particularly well placed to tell you what classes you should and should not be taking. If you tell them a little about your interests and plans, they can be even more helpful. Most professors will not mind giving this advice and will even be flattered that you want to know their

26. See Kieran Healy, "Student Evaluations," www.kieranhealy.org.

opinion and take more courses in their discipline. Note, however, that professors will be reluctant to badmouth their colleagues openly, so keep an eye out for subtle hints. If a professor doesn't mention a course or is reticent to speak about one you are interested in, that may be their way of telling you to avoid it.

TIP 22
....

Take Courses That Relate to Each Other

Students often have their most rewarding semesters when they take several courses that interrelate in synergistic ways. Often the courses have similar subjects but are taught in different departments—for example, a political science course on economic policy along with an economics course on the same subject. Or even two courses in the same department but taught by professors with different perspectives. This has several benefits. It forces you to confront multiple ways of thinking about a subject instead of the perspective of a single professor or discipline. Bringing insights from one class into another allows you to contribute more creative ideas to class discussion and write more thoughtful essays. More practically, often there is overlap in the readings for the classes, which gives you a chance to emphasize depth rather than jump around from subject to subject (the "if this is Tuesday, it must be biology" feeling).

Thinking more broadly about your academic career, another advice guide recommends putting together a "personal narrative called your transcript."[27] What they mean is that you should be able to tell a story that explains most (of course, not all) of your course choices. This is more than an explanation for your choice of major; it is an explanation that ties together a broad cross-section of your classes. For example, you might be a sociology major who focused on urban life and thus took courses in African American studies, economics, and politics, all of which focused on ways to improve cities. Having a narrative like this will not only teach you more—because of the synergies between the courses I just mentioned—but it will give you something to say to future employers who want to know that you have gotten an education rather than taken a random series of classes.

27. Peter Feaver, Sue Wasiolek, and Anne Crossman, *Getting the Best Out of College: A Professor, a Dean, and a Student Tell You How to Maximize Your Experience* (Berkeley, CA: Ten Speed Press, 2008), p. 54.

TIP 23

Study Abroad for at Least One Semester if Not an Entire Year

While universities try to be diverse, they are inevitably grounded in one place. If you are at Princeton, you are at Princeton with all the limitations that life in a small suburban New Jersey town entails. (I grew up in the town next door, so I know whereof I speak.) Further, most American universities—unlike those in foreign countries—are built around delimited campuses, the proverbial ivory tower, that tend to isolate you from the rest of the world.[28]

Indeed, a typical problem with American students is what the Princeton philosophy professor K. Anthony Appiah calls their "astonishing parochialism": "Too many of our students haven't the faintest idea what life is like anywhere outside the class and the community—let alone the country—they grew up in." While courses on other peoples and cultures may help overcome this parochialism, they are not enough.

One of the best antidotes that colleges offer to this problem is the study abroad program. As Professor Appiah puts it, "But parochialism isn't a matter of not knowing a bunch of cultural snippets about peoples everywhere. It's an attitude. And the fellow from Des Moines or San Francisco who spends a semester at Tallinn or Johannesburg or Berlin or even Canberra at least acquires the basic Another Country insight: They do things differently there."[29]

Some study abroad programs expose you to this insight better than others. A simple rule is the more foreign the better. If possible go to a country that does not speak English (don't follow the crowds to England, Scotland, Ireland, and Australia). Better yet is a non-Western country—just about anywhere in Africa or Asia. The cultural differences will be larger, and you will get a chance to test out a new language to boot. If you can, try to live with a family, which gives you more opportunities to learn about the culture. Dormitory life is pretty homogeneous the world over. Similarly, try to take classes with actual students at the university in their native tongue rather than courses set aside for foreigners. If you do go to a Western country, stay away from the large, cosmopolitan cities that are full of foreigners

28. European universities tend to be located in large cities and more integrated with the urban environment.

29. K. Anthony Appiah, "Learn Statistics, Go Abroad," *Slate*, November 15, 2005.

and choose a provincial city where you can encounter a more "authentic" or at least a more foreign culture.

No matter where you go, try to prepare in advance for your study abroad experience. If you can, take intensive language courses before you go. If you already speak a foreign language, definitely choose a country that speaks that language (though for French speakers Francophone Africa is as good a choice as France proper). Better still is to take courses in the art, culture, religion, history, and politics of the place you plan to visit. The more you know going in, the more you will take with you going out.

TIP 24

Don't Succumb to the "Two Cultures"

The phrase "two cultures" was coined by the physicist and novelist C. P. Snow to refer to the different worlds of the sciences and the humanities. He saw that the two had become increasingly disconnected in the modern world. In his own words,

> A good many times I have been present at gatherings of people who, by the standards of the traditional culture, are thought highly educated and who have with considerable gusto been expressing their incredulity at the illiteracy of scientists. Once or twice I have been provoked and have asked the company how many of them could describe the Second Law of Thermodynamics. The response was cold: it was also negative. Yet I was asking something which is about the scientific equivalent of: Have you read a work of Shakespeare's? I now believe that if I had asked an even simpler question—such as, What do you mean by mass, or acceleration, which is the scientific equivalent of saying, Can you read?—not more than one in ten of the highly educated would have felt that I was speaking the same language. So the great edifice of modern physics goes up, and the majority of the cleverest people in the western world have about as much insight into it as their neolithic ancestors would have had.[30]

Of course the knife cuts both ways. Unlike Snow, many brilliant scientists are all but ignorant of the works of Shakespeare, Plato, and other milestones of human civilization. And each side has its own smug way of looking at the

30. C. P. Snow, *The Two Cultures and the Scientific Revolution* (New York: Cambridge University Press, 1993), pp. 14–15.

other. Those in the sciences see the humanists as lacking rigor and standards, while the humanists see the scientists as lacking soul and judgment.

Most undergraduates place themselves on one or the other side of this boundary line. They are either science types and take most of their courses in fields that use equations and laboratories or they are humanistic types and focus on courses with heavy reading and writing requirements.

I think the second type is more prevalent. Too many students are afraid to take classes that use math. This is a mistake. As Professor Appiah, himself a humanist, remarks, "Many [humanities majors] don't know how to evaluate mathematical models or statistical arguments. And I think that makes you incompetent to participate in many discussions of public policy."[31] The reason is that almost all policy proposals are based on models of likely consequences that are nearly impossible to evaluate without some mathematical background. More generally, in the words of the Harvard psychology professor Steven Pinker,

> General science education, often an afterthought, needs to be reconsidered, because scientific literacy is more important than ever. It's not just essential to being a competent citizen who can understand, for example, why hydrogen fuel cannot solve energy shortages. . . . Science is also critical because it is blending with the other realms of human knowledge.
>
> One . . . example is the sciences of human nature, such as cognitive neuroscience, behavioral genetics, and evolutionary psychology. They are illuminating the mental processes that go into creating and appreciating art and that drive the social contracts underlying economic and political systems.[32]

Part of the problem is with professors. Scientists and mathematicians often don't take the first step by offering comprehensible and stimulating courses that would attract students without a background in science—both Professors Appiah and Pinker agree on this. But there is also a reluctance among students to seek out the challenges of these subjects. Indeed, in his survey of graduating seniors, Richard Light found that one of their biggest regrets was not taking more science courses.[33]

On the other side, many science and engineering majors stay away from courses that require heavy reading or writing. This is a mistake as well. These skills are necessary in just about any occupation as Tip 14 showed.

31. Appiah, "Learn Statistics, Go Abroad."
32. Steven Pinker, "The Matrix, Revisited," *Slate*, November 16, 2005.
33. Light, *Making the Most of College*, pp. 69–73.

Moreover, familiarity with the cultural life of a society is probably as necessary as technical knowledge for being a successful person much less a useful citizen. It is these classes that will teach not only what your society is, but who you are and what you truly believe. Only in encountering the great works of literature, philosophy, music, and art will you find out what it is to be human.

While this may not seem important now, you neglect it at your own risk. When your dark night of the soul comes—and it comes for just about everyone—you will be glad to have these works to find solace in. Telling is the case of John Stuart Mill. Trained by his father almost from birth in the classical languages, math, and economics—he could read Plato in the original at age ten—Mill had a nervous breakdown when he was twenty-one. He found his way out of it only when he turned to the Romantic poet Wordsworth whose verses showed him another side of the world. Mill of course became one of the greatest philosophers of modern times.

In short, it is easy to get stuck on one side of these "culture" wars, but you should resist that temptation. Even if you are bad at math or writing, you are shortchanging both yourself and society by avoiding them.

TIP 25
....

Don't Try to Get All of Your General Education Requirements Out of the Way in Freshman and Sophomore Year

Most schools have general education requirements that require you to take courses in a variety of different fields (see Tip 8). These are good things. They do something like Tip 13; they force you to take courses outside of your comfort zone.[34] But they are not a be-all and end-all. Many students assume that because these courses are requirements they need to be gotten out of the way as soon as possible.

But as George Dennis O'Brien puts it, "It hardly seems an exhilarating entrance to higher studies to spend one's initial years in getting things out of the way."[35] Your first goal in college should be to find out what fields you

---

34. The claim about these courses is that they produce well-rounded students. The joke is that like billiard balls, they roll in whatever direction they are stroked.

35. George Dennis O'Brien, *All the Essential Half-Truths about Higher Education* (Chicago: University of Chicago Press, 1998), p. 78.

CHOOSING CLASSES : 71

love and have a talent for. General education requirements can be a means to that end, but only a means. Don't take a class just because it fulfills a requirement. Take it because the topic interests you or the professor is great or it provides you with an important skill.

The benefit of postponing some distribution requirements is not only that you can better determine what you really care about early in your college career and devote more attention to that subject. It is also that as a junior or senior you can pick required courses that better complement your studies. Once you are a more experienced student you will be better able to choose courses that both satisfy requirements and provide you with useful training. This is much harder to do as a freshman who knows neither what she wants to study nor how the university works.

TIP 26
....
Audit Classes That You Don't Have Time to Take

The George Mason economist Bryan Caplan has a bit of advice for people who care only about learning rather than the credential of a diploma. He says this, "The best education in the world is already free of charge. Just go to the best university in the world and start attending classes. Stay as long as you want, and study everything that interests you. No one will ever 'card' you. The only problem is that, no matter how much you learn, there won't be any record you were ever there."[36]

You can apply his insights to life at a university. A typical student will take maybe thirty-two courses during her four-year college career—four courses per semester over eight semesters. This out of the several hundred or thousand that the university offers (my university has more than two thousand courses in the catalog that are purportedly offered regularly plus hundreds of others offered as "special topics"). You may feel that you are working hard to keep up with those thirty-two courses and all of the reading and writing that they entail. But in my experience students still have a good amount of free time, and it would be a shame not to take advantage of all the great courses being taught at a university, particularly when you are paying so much for the privilege to take them "legally."

36. See Bryan Caplan, "Get the Best Education in the World, Absolutely Free!" econlog .econlib.org.

My suggestion is to audit a course or two every quarter. Auditing means that you go to the lectures (audit is Latin for "listen"), but don't complete the assignments and don't receive a grade.[37] Sometimes this is formally noted at registration time; sometimes it is on your own initiative. In the latter case, you should typically ask the professors if they mind your sitting in. Usually they won't, but they may ask you to keep up with the reading if it is a seminar class.

In any case, your main investment is showing up for the three hours a week when the class meets and perhaps doing an occasional reading that interests you. The payoff, however, is large—you get to absorb all of the professor's hard work in preparing the lectures and organizing the material. It seems like a good deal to me and lets you sample far more of the university's enormous offerings than the thirty-some courses you take for credit. Indeed, you will sometimes meet professors doing the same thing.

TIP 27

Consider Independent Study Classes

At some point in the career of ambitious college students, they have either learned about all they can from the courses offered in their field or discovered topics that are not well covered by existing course offerings. When this happens, you should be proactive and start to create your own courses. Most universities allow students to do this through independent study classes.

This does not mean going off and studying by yourself, but instead creating an actual syllabus and set of assignments that you proceed to complete under the supervision of a professor. This gives you the freedom to focus on things you care about and to forge a relationship with a professor with whom you will be meeting personally several times during the course of the semester. And since most independent study classes culminate in a research project, you have the opportunity to produce original scholarship and learn by doing rather than hearing (see Tip 43).

You need to be careful in approaching professors to supervise your course. Many professors are skeptical of independent study classes because they fear that students won't devote serious effort to them and because it means extra work for which they are usually not compensated. You need to make the

---

37. This is a cheaper alternative to the tapes of "great lectures" mentioned earlier.

case that you are a serious student who is not taking this lightly. You are on firmest ground when you address a professor who both knows you well and is an expert on the subject you want to study. In all cases, you should prepare a preliminary syllabus before you visit the professor. Determine what the main works you want to read are. Outline the research project you want to undertake and your timeline for completing it. Then ask for advice on what else the professor thinks you should read or do. A demonstration of your seriousness of purpose along with an interesting topic that is not covered by existing course offerings will help to persuade professors that you deserve their mentorship.

TIP 28

Don't Take Too Many Classes with One Professor

Students often fall in love (I hope not literally) with one of their professors and wish to take all of their classes with him or her. While it is not a bad idea to take an additional class with a professor you know is good and whom you would like to know better, there are also disadvantages. In my own case, students can imbibe most of my wisdom in the course of a semester. During the second class, I start to repeat myself—if not my exact words and examples, at least my general philosophy (and certainly my jokes). It is important to sample as much wisdom as you can at university, so it is a good idea to try a variety of professors. Of course, if one of us seems to you an unending font of wisdom, by all means help yourself to another cup.

TIP 29

Don't Be Afraid to Exceed Requirements

The idea behind requirements, both general education ones and majors, is that on their own students will not get a broad enough or deep enough education. They might specialize too narrowly or skim the surface too much. But remember that requirements are only trying to ensure a minimum of breadth and depth. There is no reason why you should merely fulfill requirements. Feel free to go beyond the official requirements—take extra courses in your major or overfulfill distribution requirements. Don't assume that wise social planners have manufactured these requirements to produce the perfect education; they have not. Requirements are there (hopefully) to correct some of students' biases in course selection—their tendency to stick with the familiar and easy—not to ensure that everyone gets what they need. Only you know the answer to that question, and requirements are at best an imperfect guide.

TIP 30
....

Unless You Plan to Major in Chemistry or Biology, Leave Medical School Requirements until Later

It is hard to overemphasize how many students start college as pre-med, take all eight semesters of required courses (four chemistry, two biology, and two physics), and only then realize that they don't wish to become a doctor. (I was one of these.) About a quarter of students show up as freshman thinking that they are pre-med, but only a handful end up going to medical school. Almost everyone drops their initial plan after taking two, four, six, or eight semesters of courses that they would not otherwise take and which they rarely remember with fondness. If you think that this does not apply to you, then think again.

Why so many freshmen believe they need to prepare for medical school is a bit of a mystery to me. The reasons are typically vague. "I want to help others" is the most common one I hear. But what do other professions do, hurt people? I would guess that the underlying reasons are a failure of imagination—few freshmen have any idea of the possible careers they may pursue—the seduction of the high esteem in which doctors are held (and the high salaries they receive as a consequence), and lack of confidence in their ability to forge their own career path. But it is usually not long before most students abandon these ideas.

The question is whether they abandon their pre-med plans before or after spending a quarter of their education (almost the equivalent of another major) on courses for which they have little alternative use. I would add that many of these courses are designed only for pre-med students, not for teaching the particular science as it should be taught. Physics departments, for example, typically have a watered-down version of physics for pre-med students and another for those truly interested in physics.[38] The pre-med

---

38. The pre-med version uses algebra instead of calculus, which makes the concepts even harder to understand.

version is designed entirely around the MCAT (Medical College Admissions Test), not the principles of physics.

I would thus advise students to defer their pre-med courses until they are fairly certain that they wish to become doctors. It is easy enough to take the required courses in summer programs or after college. If you are convinced that they need to be completed during your undergraduate career, put them off to junior and senior year when you are convinced that medical school is for you. By this time, you will have sampled many other fields and learned a little more about other career possibilities (see Tip 70). More likely you will simply become confident enough in your own abilities that you no longer need the safety net of a predefined career like medicine or law.

TIP 31

Either Take Foreign Language Classes Seriously or Try to Place Out of Them

Many universities have a foreign language requirement, usually one or two years of a particular language. The problem with these requirements is that they are neither here nor there. Unless you have good prior training, you don't learn enough of a language to use it with facility, but the requirement is burdensome enough that it does detract from your education. Or as George Dennis O'Brien puts it, you learn "enough French to order from the menu, not enough to compliment the chef."[39]

My advice is to push through this requirement to the next level. Do try to become fluent in a foreign language. This means starting the foreign language at the most advanced level you can, exceeding university requirements, and attending a study abroad program in a country that uses the language you study.

This may seem extreme, but graduating students say that their language classes were among their most satisfying.[40] The reason is that they closely approximate the kind of teaching that I have advocated here. They are taught in small sections, feature a lot of student participation, require daily assignments, and provide loads of feedback on your progress. This is what

---

39. O'Brien, *All the Essential Half-Truths about Higher Education*, p. 80.

40. Light, *Making the Most of College*, pp. 77–80. Alumni concur on this. They are strong advocates of continued foreign language requirements.

you should be seeking in all of your classes, but foreign language classes actually provide it. And this is not to mention the most important point: that you will gain a lifelong skill that will both broaden your horizons and help you practically.

If, however, you believe that you are unable to push through to a higher level—I am suspicious of this; a majority of human beings speak more than one language—then don't waste your time in introductory Spanish. A low-level introduction to a foreign language will not get you very far, and you would be better off devoting those hours to other pursuits. If this is your case, then try to place out of these requirements. This is a second-best solution, but is still better than a perfunctory acquaintance with a foreign language. If you decide to do this though, do seek out courses about foreign cultures to make up for your lack of language training.

TIP 32

Be Discerning in Choosing Internships for Credit

Some universities offer students the opportunity to take internships for credit. If they are well designed, internships can be an excellent way of learning, often better than a classroom experience because you learn by actually doing something. You also get a sense of a particular career and whether it is the right one for you (see Tip 70). Students tend to be woefully uninformed about the sorts of jobs out there and the skills needed to succeed in them. Research has shown that internship experience helps students develop more career-related skills and makes them more employable.

My worry is that many internships have you doing secretarial or clerical work or little work at all. They are not designed to teach much less challenge you, but to make a profit off of your tuition dollars or take advantage of your free labor.[41] This is not to say that even just hanging around a profession you are interested in can't be worthwhile; it can, even if only to show you that it is not the one for you. But do consider whether an internship will actually allow you to engage in substantive tasks. Do the same sort of preliminary research on an internship that you would do before taking a class at college.

41. Sonia Smith, "Biting the Hand That Doesn't Feed Me: Internships for College Credit Are a Scam," *Slate*, June 8, 2006.

TIP 33

....

Take Prerequisites with a Grain of Salt

Many classes require you to take certain prerequisites before you enroll. The idea is that you already need to know certain things to make sense of the course material. These requirements, however, are more a word to the wise than a definitive judgment. It is a professor's way of saying: I am not going to hold your hand if you don't understand the concepts. That said, if you don't think you need the prerequisite, then go ahead and take the class. Why should you waste your limited course budget on classes you prefer not to take? Explaining to the professor your reasons for wanting to take the class and your commitment to work hard are usually enough for you to be allowed to enroll.

TIP 34

....

Consider Graduate Courses

As chapter 8 describes, graduate school is quite different than undergraduate study. Students are typically highly motivated and willing to work very hard. Professors in turn devote more attention to graduate students and push them harder (see Rule C in chapter 9). Both circumstances lead to a much more intense academic experience than undergraduate study. Class discussion sparkles, assignments come fast and heavy, and feedback is constant. Plus only full-time tenure-track professors are teaching these classes.

For all these reasons, you may wish to sample some graduate classes in fields that you know well. You should expect these classes to be hard, and you should not expect special treatment because you are an undergrad. There is relatively little hand-holding; those who can't keep up are left by the wayside. But if you feel ready for them—the undergraduate curriculum is no longer challenging you—then a graduate course will provide a better and more concentrated learning experience.

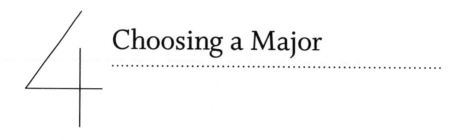

Choosing a Major

In educational systems outside of the United States, students enter university with a field already chosen. Usually they apply to and are accepted by not a university but a specific department or "faculty" at the university, and they take most of their courses in that department. They are more a student at, say, the Department of Philosophy than the university as a whole. The American system is different. It assumes that students are more or less tabulae rasae (blank slates), that they come to college with little idea of what they can or should study.

The university major is an attempt to steer between the Scylla of complete concentration in a particular field (the European style) and the Charybdis of no specialization (a chimera that exists at no university).[1] It was invented at Harvard in the early part of the twentieth century after an experiment with no required courses, which itself followed the old style of a nearly comprehensive mandatory curriculum.[2] The major was intended to give students some specialized knowledge while leaving them room to try out new things at the same time.

In this chapter, I am going to take these American tendencies to heart and assume that you really do come to university as a tabula rasa. In fact, given the state of our high schools, you probably should. University education is very different from high school education (high schools might benefit from becoming more like universities) and will expose you to very different ways

1. Schools that appear to offer no structure at all, like Brown, usually have a strong advising system that helps students to construct a structured course of study, but a structure that is created by the student.

2. When Harvard experimented with no required courses, most students ended up taking only introductory courses. See Charles McGrath, "What Every Student Needs to Know," *New York Times*, January 8, 2006.

of thinking and learning. For this reason, you should avoid choosing a specialization in your first year of college. Let the system work its magic on you.

But then do think seriously about your choice of major. A recent *New York Times* survey found that the second largest regret of recent graduates—following only the regret that they had played too much—was choosing the wrong major.[3] One in six (16 percent) respondents said that they would have chosen a different major if they had it to do over again. It is the intention of this chapter to avert exactly those regrets.

Once you have chosen your major, keep in mind that there are four things you should take away from it.[4] You should acquire a body of knowledge about a particular subject: what scholars have discovered. You should learn the standard methods of inquiry in your field: the ways that scholars gather information. You should gain the skills to analyze and process this information. And finally, you should get practice using these abilities to solve complicated problems in the field. Try to make sure that your major provides you with all of these things.

TIP 35

Sample a Lot of Different Departments

American universities assume that students arrive with little idea about the broad range of human knowledge that can be studied. Fields like astronomy, linguistics, philosophy, art history, foreign literature, statistics, sociology, economics, and African American studies—to name just a few—are among those rarely taught in any depth in high schools. Even those that are taught regularly—history, English, biology, chemistry, physics, and math—look far different at the university level.

For this reason, it is imperative that you sample from a large number of different departments. Departments differ not just in subject matter, but in the ways they study the world. They may use mathematical models or field research. They may carry out close readings or viewings of classic texts. They may conduct lab experiments or even rely on self-introspection. It would be ideal to pursue all of these modes of knowing, but four years gives

3. *New York Times* Alumni Poll, June 15–23, 2007.
4. See Derek Bok, *Our Underachieving Colleges: A Candid Look at How Much Students Learn and Why They Should Be Learning More* (Princeton, NJ: Princeton University Press, 2006), p. 137.

you only so much time.[5] What is best is to try a number of them to determine both what fascinates you and what you do well.

Try not to rule out any fields in advance. Many students turn on a dime when exposed to new subjects. Artsy students may discover astronomy and decide to learn the math they need to get them through. Students who can't speak a foreign language may decide to major in Russian after reading Dostoyevsky. Computer geeks may be seduced by the austere logic of analytic philosophy. There are no boring subjects, only bored people. The right teacher can make a subject like tropical insects or Greek drama seem like the only thing that matters in the world and turn you into a budding entomologist or classicist.

TIP 36

Choose a Major That You Love

If there is a time in your life when you can and should pursue something simply because you love it, college is that time. If you love watching the stars, digging for archeological finds, reading great literature, searching for the meaning of life, or composing symphonies, you should by all means take as many courses in those subjects as you can swallow. After college your chances to pursue these fields—much less pursue them with the guidance of acknowledged and caring experts—drop considerably. Unfortunately, there are not as many jobs for astronomers, archeologists, literary critics, philosophers, and composers as there should be. Yes, learning can and should be a lifelong endeavor, but when you take on real life responsibilities, you often find that you have neither the time nor the energy to pursue what you really love. College is your main chance to study the thing you love, and it would be a shame if you didn't take it.

While some students believe that they must choose a "practical" major, few academic majors are really practical (see Tip 38). Unless you choose a vocational field like journalism, accounting, or engineering, your education will not be particularly useful in an obvious way. More important, whatever major you choose will not handicap you too much in a future career. The

5. The Department of Education's Classification of Instructional Programs includes nine hundred different majors. The 2009 *College Board Book of Majors* (New York: College Board, 2008) describes 195 of them in depth.

beauty of the U.S. economy is that art history majors can be investment bankers and math majors can run art galleries. You aren't judged by your major, but by what you can do.[6] (This is not as true in other countries where your course of study often tracks you into a particular career.)

I would add that the more you love the subject you study, the harder you will work at it and the better you will do. Research has shown that experts are not born, but made.[7] Even if you have great natural talent in a subject, you will not be a star without working hard at it. Some scholars have postulated a ten-thousand-hour rule—that is the number of hours you need to devote to a skill in order to achieve mastery.[8] Virtually all of the great geniuses—from Mozart to Michael Jordan—worked like dogs to make themselves great; it didn't just come naturally. And to work like a dog, you have to love what you are doing. If you don't love it, you won't go the extra mile that separates the good from the great. You will be far more successful if you choose a major that you really care about than if you choose one for other reasons.

This is not to say that you must love every course you take in your major. But you should at least feel fascinated by the questions they are asking. This or that professor may disappoint you, but you should always find solace in the material you are studying. Doing what you love is the best route to becoming an academic star.

6. Studies have found that business majors do earn about 10 percent more than others, but this effect lasts only about ten years. See Bok, *Our Underachieving Colleges*, p. 295.

7. Stephen J. Dubner and Steven D. Levitt, "Experts Are Made and Practice Matters, but Birthdays Matter Too," *New York Times*, May 7, 2006.

8. It is not mere practice, but constant striving to be better in those hours that matters. See Malcolm Gladwell, *Outliers: The Story of Success* (New York: Little, Brown and Company, 2008). The idea is from Herbert Simon and Anders Ericsson.

SOME NEGLECTED MAJORS

Far be it from me to judge the fields of my colleagues. Yes, I do have opinions on other fields—which are more worthy of study and which less—but in the interest of collegiality I won't share those opinions with you here. What I would do is point out a few majors that I think have been unjustly neglected, which more students would choose and enjoy if they only considered them more seriously.

Linguistics. A major in linguistics is not a major in a foreign language. In fact, some of the most renowned linguists speak only one language. What it is is the study of language itself. If you have opinions on whether English is in decline, whether some languages are harder than others, or whether the language you speak affects the way you think, this may be the field for you. As Steven Pinker puts it, "I have never met a person who is not interested in language." Moreover, in the past several decades the field has made enormous progress so that we now know a lot about how language works and how people use it. (Don't confuse linguists with the pseudo-grammarians who bemoan the way Americans use apostrophes.) In a knowledge economy like the United States that relies so fundamentally on language, there are real payoffs from being schooled in linguistics. If you want to be even more intrigued by the field, pick up some recent popular books on linguistics like Steven Pinker's *The Language Instinct*, Laurie Bauer and Peter Trudgill's *Language Myths*, or Geoffrey Nunberg's *Going Nucular*. And then go take courses in it.

Regional studies majors. Most students take a language class or two at college, usually because it is required. But not enough people seriously consider majors like Slavic studies, European studies, African studies, Latin American studies, or Middle Eastern studies. These majors teach you not only an extra language or two, but also knowledge of the politics, economics, society, and culture of a foreign country or region. As the world becomes more globalized at all levels, such knowledge will begin to yield greater benefits in your future career. Moreover these majors give students an impressive combination of depth and breadth—depth in learning in detail about a single culture or region and breadth in taking courses in a wide variety of different departments ranging from history to anthropology to economics to literature. I am still amazed that even after the fate of the United States has intersected with the Middle East in such dramatic ways, few students have taken up the challenge of studying the region in all its dimensions.

Sociology. Some of the most interesting questions in the current world are being asked in sociology. While the field has a reputation for left-wing activism and sometimes crazy causes, most departments possess a core of faculty who study the social world in a rigorous and analytical manner. And the number of interesting phenomena they study is nearly infinite; almost nothing that is human escapes their purview. From how drug dealers manage their subordinates and how your friends influence your weight to the way economists create as well as study markets and the sort of societies formed among Facebook members, recent works in sociology have pursued all of these questions. If you want to get a hold on many of the forces shaping the world today, you may find what you are looking for in sociology.

Statistics. To fully understand just about any phenomenon in the world, from atoms to people to countries, you need a grasp of statistics. Statistics teaches you how to measure quantities, collect data, and then draw inferences from that information. Though this might sound boring, these tasks are necessary to explain most of the forces affecting our lives. If you want to know how H1N1 will spread, how to pick better investments, and who will win the next presidential election, then statistics are your best hope for finding an answer. A statistics major is also extremely marketable; Google's chief economist calls it the "sexy job" of the next decade. There is hardly a firm which could not benefit from a trained statistician, and statisticians are just as desirable for public interest groups hoping to help the disadvantaged. And if you worry that you are not the math type, statistics is considerably more applied than a pure math major and does more to help you understand the real world in all its complexities.

TIP 37

Find Out What You Are Good At

People do well at the things they like, but they also like the things they do well. I took a course in economics on a lark, but was told by a professor that I had a real talent for the subject and ended up majoring in it. So, one way to identify a major is to find out what you do well.

How do you know where your talents lie? This is not always easy to find out. In the first place, there are dozens of subjects available for study. Tip 35 already suggested that you try a lot of different departments. At the most basic level this will show you what you feel confident in doing. You will sense that in certain subjects you have a greater understanding of the material and your assignments are easier and more pleasurable to complete. These are signs that you are good at these things.

You will also receive signals from your professors about your talents. Grades are one of the main signals. Indeed, one of the fundamental purposes of grades is to tell you what you do well and what you do less well (see text box on "What Grades Mean"). An A means you are doing something well, a C not so much.

Unfortunately, grades are fuzzy signals. In the first place, grading is not a science. Maybe your professor didn't like you. Or you were sick on the day of the final. And it is hard to sum up all of your abilities and potential abilities in a single letter.

A more systematic problem is that different professors grade in different ways.[9] Professors in one department may give mostly As, and those in another mostly Cs. So when you get a B+, does that mean you have below average talents (as in the department that gives mostly As) or above average talents (as in the department that gives mostly Cs)? Unless you know where you rank relative to other students, it is hard to tell where your talents lie.

How do you find out how you are doing relative to others? You might simply ask other students in the class what sort of grades they received, or you might get a general feeling for whether a professor or department is perceived as hard or easy grading. As an approximate rule, science and math departments tend to give lower grades than humanities departments, but there are often exceptions depending on the department's culture.[10] Better still is to try to get personalized feedback from your professors. They may provide this without prompting—encouraging you to take more courses and praising your talents—or you can visit their office hours. Ask them pointedly how you compare to other students at a similar point in their academic career. They should be able to tell you whether you are more or less talented in the subject than the average student.

It is tempting to choose a major that gives higher grades because you will end up with a higher GPA. But even if you choose a hard-grading department, there are ways to signal to graduate schools and employers that you took a harder road and thus your GPA is lower than it might have been otherwise. Most employers already have a sense of how things work: that, for example, physicists tend to be tougher graders than art historians. The

9. See Richard Sabot and John Wakeman-Linn, "Grade Inflation and Course Choice," *Journal of Economic Perspectives* 5, no. 1 (1989): 159–70. The authors note that since students are more likely to take another course in the same subject if they receive a high grade, high grading departments will tend to attract more majors. They attribute the decline in science majors to the fact that science departments tend to give low grades.

10. Small departments often give higher grades as well in order to attract students. This advice may thus be in tension with Tip 39.

hard-grading department that I graduated from offered a special note that students could attach to their transcript explaining that their lower grades were partly a consequence of department policy. Even better would be to encourage universities to put the average grade for each class on students' transcripts. Regardless of what your university does, in the long run you will be better served by studying what you do well than by what promises you the highest GPA.

TIP 38

Don't Worry Too Much about the Job Prospects of the Major

Students often want to know the real-world applications of different majors; what jobs a particular major will help them find. If you are getting a liberal arts education—as most readers of this book probably are—this question does not make much sense. The idea of this education—and in a recent survey over 90 percent of professors agreed on this—is to teach students how to think critically.[11] In other words, to understand and analyze arguments—to see their strengths and weaknesses—and to construct original arguments. The principle behind this emphasis is that such skills can be taught in just about any field—whether literature, math, or political science—and that they will be applicable to just about any field of endeavor you choose after graduation.

In fact, few liberal arts majors prepare you for a job (except perhaps for a job as a professor). Some of the natural sciences or computer science may give you the skills for an entry-level job as a lab assistant or programmer; economics might give you a leg up in the race for jobs in investment banking; but in general none of these majors gives you vocational training for a particular task. Fortunately, in America not only are universities structured to give you an impractical education, but American business is set up the same way. Most industries expect you to learn on the job, not to come already prepared. They would prefer to hire a brilliant and creative English major over an indifferent economics major. A recent *New York Times* survey found that only about half of recent graduates of three selective colleges were working in the field they studied.[12] In short, don't be too caught up in the relevance of your major.

11. Bok, *Our Underachieving Colleges*, pp. 67–68 .
12. *New York Times* Alumni Poll, June 15–23, 2007.

Of course, don't ignore it altogether. There are significant salary differences between different majors. Economics and engineering majors, for example, tend to earn considerably more than art history majors. But as the economist Daniel Hamermesh puts it, "once you account for the longer hours worked by business and engineering majors, by the fact that they often have higher SAT scores, and other factors, the differences are much smaller; indeed, over half of the variation in earnings by major disappears."[13] In short, given who you are—that is, how smart and hardworking you are—the major you choose will not add too much to your earning potential. So why not study what you love?

TIP 39

Choose Smaller Majors

In an ideal world, universities would keep a rough balance between the number of faculty in a department and the number of students the department teaches. They would make sure that students got the same amount of personal attention no matter what major they chose. But the relation is far from precise. Course enrollments fluctuate, faculty cannot be hired and fired at will, and there is a minimum number of faculty for a department to be viable. For these reasons and others, some departments may be drowning in students, and others may be hungry for them.[14] At Harvard, for example, each economics professor is responsible for sixteen majors, while in the Slavic and German departments there are more faculty members than majors.

These differences can have a large effect on your education. In a department that is understaffed relative to demand, you are less likely to have close contact with faculty and more likely to be stuck in large lecture classes.

13. See Daniel Hamermesh, "Which Majors Make the Most?" freakonomics.blogs .nytimes.com. The results are from Daniel S. Hamermesh and Stephen G. Donald, "The Effect of College Curriculum on Earnings: An Affinity Identifier for Non-Ignorable Non-Response Bias," University of Texas at Austin, working paper.

14. Two economists found a number of determinants of a department's student-faculty ratio. Departments with higher salaries and higher research productivity have higher student-faculty ratios, while smaller departments have lower ratios. They also suggest that university politics play an important role. See William R. Johnson and Sarah Turner, "Faculty without Students: Resource Allocation in Higher Education," *Journal of Economic Perspectives* 23, no. 2 (Spring 2009): 169–89.

There will also be more competition for places in popular classes, RA jobs, and department awards. This is reversed in a department that has many faculty members but few students. Such departments will go the extra mile to attract students by emphasizing teaching and personalized interactions. These departments will give you more attention both inside and outside the classroom, allowing you to participate more deeply in the life of the department.

It is not easy to find out where these imbalances lie. A recent study found that political science, economics, and psychology have very high student-faculty ratios (bad for you), while some humanities like religion, classics, and foreign languages and some hard sciences like physics and mathematics have low ratios (good for you). You can get a sense of these differences by seeing whether a department offers more large lecture classes or small seminars. A simpler rule is that larger departments (that is, departments with more professors) have higher student-faculty ratios than smaller departments, but this is not always the case. Note, however, that there may be countervailing forces. It may be that popular departments are doing something right that allows them to attract so many students.

The more general version of this tip is to look for departments that offer more personalized interactions. The ratio of students to faculty is one way of determining this, but it is not the only one. Simply keep your eye out for departments that are run like families and avoid those that are run like factories. While this should not be your main consideration in choosing a major—loving the subject is the first prerequisite and having some facility for it the second—it should certainly play a part in your calculus.

TIP 40

Choose More Structured Majors

Majors differ in the amount of structure they provide to students. Some require students simply to take any ten courses in the subject. Others have a clearly defined sequence of courses that students are required to take. All else equal, you should prefer majors that lean toward the second model. More structure means that the designers of the major have put more thought into what they would like you to take away from your studies. They wish to ensure that all students have a grasp of the central ideas and methods of the subject. At the end of a major, you should be able to think like a philosopher or sociologist or chemist; you should know the way that your field approaches problems and be able to handle complex problems in the field by yourself. Structured majors tend to foster these abilities more than unstructured ones.

What are the signs of a structured major? There should be a sequence of courses that gradually builds up a set of skills so that later courses use the skills accumulated in the earlier ones rather than reinventing the wheel at every turn. Numerous prerequisites in higher-level courses are a sign of this. Structured majors also have a set of courses that all majors are required to take rather than multiple choices at each level. This is the core knowledge they want you to take away. Finally, structured majors culminate in a large project like a senior thesis or oral exam that ensures that students use their new-found skills in a way that stretches their abilities.

This is not to say that you should judge all majors by their degree of structure. One of the reasons that certain majors lack structure is that the field itself is divided about what constitutes its core insights and methods.[15] In short, professors can't agree on what students should be taught. These majors may not be bad—particularly, if you care deeply about the subject— but there is a greater risk that you will leave them feeling confused about what the field is trying to do. And while confusion can be productive for the more intellectually mature, it is usually better to develop a clear idea of what you have learned.

15. All fields are divided in some ways. What matters is how contested these divisions are. Truly divided departments tend not to serve their students well. They have difficulty constructing a coherent major, providing a collegial learning environment, and even hiring new faculty members.

WOMEN AND THE SCIENCES

Women were once completely absent from universities. Today most universities enroll more women than men. While women are typically as successful as their male counterparts (at least as far as grades go), they still face obstacles in certain areas. One of the most prominent is in the fields of science, technology, engineering, and math. Women are 37 percent less likely to get science and engineering BAs than men.* These fields tend to be dominated by men at both the student and faculty

* National Science Foundation, "Science and Engineering Degrees: 1966–2004," National Science Foundation, Division of Science Resources Statistics, January 2007.

levels (though to be fair there are other fields or at least subfields where women are more prominent than men).

Why is this so?† Women clearly do not lack the talent to succeed in these fields. At least through high school, there is almost no gender difference in math and science ability or performance. What changes in college? While we still don't know the answer to this question, a recent study discovered one interesting trend: women tend to perform far better in math and science classes when those classes are taught by female professors.‡ Their grades are higher, and they are more likely to pursue future courses in that field. (Interestingly, the professor's gender does not affect the performance of male students.)

The reasons for this are unclear—maybe women professors teach differently or maybe they serve as role models. (The authors of the study believe that it is mainly the teaching style because some male professors are very effective in teaching women.) In either case, if you are a woman and determined not to be excluded from these fields, the advice is clear: seek out math and science classes taught by female professors and choose universities that employ more female mathematicians and scientists.

† For a fascinating debate on this point, see "The Science of Gender and Science: Pinker vs. Spelke, a Debate," *Edge*, www.edge.org, May 16, 2005.

‡ See Scott E. Carrell, Marianne E. Page, and James E. West, "Sex and Science: How Professor Gender Perpetuates the Gender Gap," NBER Working Paper No. 14959, May 2009.

TIP 41

Go to an Academic Lecture Given in the Department

Virtually every department in the university invites outside speakers to give lectures on their research. This is a formal ritual among academics where we subject our latest research to the criticism of our peers.[16] Most of the attendees at these talks will be professors and graduate students, but the talks are almost always open to the general public, and you should consider attending.

While the intellectual level of these talks may be over your head, they

16. Most departments also host job talks, which are lectures by professors the department is considering hiring. These can be just as interesting.

can give you a better idea of what the field is really about than your actual classes. They feature professors in their natural habitat doing what they were trained to do. At these talks you will discover what questions the field regards as important, what methods practitioners use to answer them, and what sort of answers they come up with. While you may never interact with this level of the field—you might catch glimpses of it in your upper-division classes—these lectures will tell you whether its questions and methods inspire you or not. If they seem trivial and unexciting, then maybe the major is not for you; if they strike you as a clever and important, you may have found a home.[17]

There is another benefit to following this tip. Because so few undergraduates attend these lectures, your presence will show the department faculty that you are a student worth taking seriously. If you are particularly intrigued by a talk, you can ask a question afterward and possibly even get invited to meet personally with the speaker. The only thing holding you back is your own reticence. A final bonus is that many of these talks are accompanied by refreshments and sometimes even lunch.[18]

TIP 42

Be Skeptical about Double or Triple Majoring

Ambitious students typically seek as many credentials as they can get. If everyone has to do one major, then they will do two. They are doing twice as much as is necessary. Does this make sense? Perhaps. The idea of a major field is to prevent students from becoming a jack of all trades and master of none. Most academic fields have a set of questions and distinct methods for addressing them. Majoring in a field gets you intimately acquainted with these questions and methods.

Does that mean that double majoring teaches you twice as much? I am not so sure. It is all to the good to study in depth as many subjects as you can. You should be taking as many upper-level courses as you can handle (see Tip 16). But you need to balance your search for depth with your search

---

17. Note that all cutting edge research is on fairly narrow topics. Vanishingly few professors are working on general theories of everything.

18. This makes them popular with graduate students who always know when food is being served.

for variety. A double major locks in over half of your courses in two departments, and this is not including other requirements.

You will thus be unable to take many electives, to simply try new fields that interest you or challenge your preconceptions. This is an important part of the college experience since college is one of the last opportunities you will have to simply take a flyer on a new subject. When else will you have the chance to study fractal geometry, premodern culture, or Romantic poetry with world-class experts? I would add that double majors do not necessarily impress graduate schools or future employers. They do not view you as doubly qualified.

If you care passionately about two different fields, a double major may be for you. But if you end up signing up for a lot of courses that you would not otherwise take simply in order to fulfill the requirements for a second major, then you might ask yourself whether it is worth it.

TIP 43
....
Write a Senior Thesis

Most colleges and universities allow and in some cases require students to write a senior or honors thesis. A senior thesis is a year-long research project that a student pursues under the guidance of a faculty member. The student comes up with a substantive research question, gathers evidence, constructs an argument, and writes up his or her conclusions in a longish paper.

I highly recommend writing a senior thesis. Doing research is a far more natural way of learning than the lectures or seminars that you normally take. There are thus considerable benefits to getting involved in real research of your own.

Consider the words of Berkeley professor Alison Gopnik:

I'm a cognitive scientist who is also a university professor. There is a staggering contrast between what I know about learning from the lab and the way I teach in the classroom. I know that human beings are designed to learn as part of their deepest evolutionary inheritance. I know that children, and even adults, learn about the everyday world around them in much the way that scientists learn. I even know something about the procedures that allow children and scientists to learn so much. They include close observation of real phenomena, active experimental investigation, and a process of guided apprenticeship. Children, and novice scientists, carefully try to imitate their mentors, and their mentors carefully watch and correct them.

Almost none of this happens in the average university classroom, including mine. . . . This is particularly ironic because modern universities have become the home of science and scholarship. And yet, notoriously, research is divorced from teaching. Faculty immersed in research think teaching is a distracting chore, and students are increasingly taught by academic lumpenproletariat adjuncts who don't do research. Students only get to do real research themselves in graduate school. What would French cooking be like if aspiring chefs never cracked an egg till after they had listened to four years of lectures about egg-cracking?[19]

While you can get something of the research experience in ordinary classes that require a research paper, it is often perfunctory and hurried. Because you are taking a full load of courses, all of which require reading and exams, your research projects typically get crammed into the last week or two of the semester, not the ideal time for reasoned thought.

You get two opportunities to pursue research in college free of these constraints. One is to become a research assistant to a professor, something I will discuss in Tip 60. But in this case, you sometimes become a gopher for the professor rather than an independent scholar. The other opportunity is writing a senior thesis. This is really the only chance you will have as an undergraduate to give sustained attention to a single topic of your own choosing over a long period without many of the responsibilities of a normal class; in fact, the senior thesis usually counts as a class in itself and does not have many requirements except writing the thesis.

Most students find the senior thesis the most challenging and rewarding part of their studies. They are forced to utilize all of the skills they have gathered over the course of their college career. Rather than spitting back material they have been taught, they have to make sense of a bewildering array of information as they try to reason their way toward the truth. And the exercise culminates with a product of real consequence that students can carry with them their whole lives—an original contribution to human knowledge.

Another benefit of the senior thesis is the opportunity to get to know a faculty member more personally. Thesis writers are typically assigned a faculty mentor. Your mentor should meet with you several times a semester, read your work, and keep an eye on your progress. Usually they will get to

19. Alison Gopnik, "Let Them Solve Problems," *Slate*, November 16, 2005.

know you well, and you will get to know them, a connection lacking in most other courses.

If you do decide to write a senior thesis, it is best to get started early. The summer before senior year, if not earlier, is the best time to begin digging into your material. Some universities even offer students grants to begin their research. Alternatively, you may be able to work as an RA for a professor in order to gain experience and develop new ideas.

The biggest challenge I have noticed in senior theses is coming up with a good research question. If you have chosen a question that is too broad, poorly specified, or even tautological (it answers itself), it will literally be impossible to write a good thesis. But a well-formed question can put you on a promising research path. There are plenty of guides in most academic subjects about not only choosing a topic, but organizing your project from start to finish. (See the recommended reading at the conclusion of the book.) In addition to following the advice in these guides, I recommend listening closely to your professors. They will give you criticisms of your ideas and may even suggest a different topic. If your professor has substantial doubts, take them very seriously. Students who write award-winning, publishable theses are usually those who have followed the advice of their professors very closely.

This is not to say that everyone should write a senior thesis. For it to be successful, you have to be a self-starter. You will set most of your own deadlines and be on your own most of the time. If you are the type who needs constant encouragement and typically leaves things to the last minute, your thesis will not turn out well. But if you are hardworking and motivated, it will likely be the most educational and memorable part of your college experience.

TIP 44

Don't Get Too Stressed Out over Your Choice

Don't beat yourself over the head about your choice of major. It is less important than you think. Since few majors prepare you for a particular career, you can go from just about any major to any career. For example, I teach a subject, political science, which I never studied (not one course) as an undergraduate. Studies have also shown that particular majors don't produce larger or smaller gains in critical thinking ability, the main skill you want to take away from college.[20] In fact, students make the most progress in critical thinking during freshman and sophomore year before they begin their major.

You also have the opportunity to change your major. In fact, there are practical advantages to declaring a major early even if you are not sure about your choice. Majors usually get first dibs in registering for oversubscribed courses in their department. Don't, however, take this temporary and opportunistic commitment as permanent. Remind yourself often that if you begin to dislike the major and prefer something else, you can and should switch. Most college majors can be theoretically completed in about three semesters. Until senior year, therefore, you have some freedom to change your decision. In short, choose something that you enjoy and can do with reasonable facility and you will have chosen well.

20. Ernest T. Pascarella and Patrick T. Terenzini, *How College Affects Students*, vol. 2, *A Third Decade of Research* (San Francisco: Jossey-Bass, 2005), pp. 65–66.

Being Successful

I have tried to distinguish this book from other guides by not focusing on subjects like study skills and getting higher grades.[1] The idea has been to give you a professor's-eye view of a university. Yet, since professors are the ones giving out grades, I should probably say something about our perspective on the subject. It is about what you would expect if you put yourself in our shoes for a moment (something that few students do).

I would add that getting good grades is related but not equivalent to learning the material and getting the most out of college. Just about anyone willing to spend all their free hours studying can get straight As. But an A merely means that you have jumped over those hurdles a professor erects because she knows that students will slack off without them. Grades do not measure learning. They measure your ability to navigate a series of sometimes arbitrary exercises. While trying to get good grades may produce learning as a by-product, it is not the royal road to that end. Success in college is not measured in GPA but in what you become and what you can do. Nevertheless, here follows some advice on being successful in a more earthly way.

TIP 45

Manage Your Time

While hard work does not guarantee you success in college, it almost always prevents failure. The toughest thing about selective colleges is getting in.

---

1. For a more thorough view on getting good grades, see Lynn F. Jacobs and Jeremy S. Hyman, *Professors' Guide to Getting Good Grades in College* (New York: Harper Collins, 2006).

Once you get in, you need to make a determined effort to fail out. With a little bit of effort, it is not hard to get reasonable grades. Today's professors typically only give out failing grades or even Ds or low Cs to students who do not complete the required assignments or devote little attention to the class. Do your work and do it conscientiously and on time and most professors will reward you with a grade in the B range.

The real problems in selective schools show up only with students who do not learn to manage their time. They never devote large blocks of time to studying.[2] They try to sneak in five minutes of studying here and ten minutes there, always in between other activities. This is a recipe for poor performance.

The key to success is to set aside several hours each day that you devote fully to your classes. Find a quiet place where you are comfortable and won't be disturbed and work on your assignments. It may be a carrel in the library, your dorm room, or a quiet café. It is as simple as that. If you have trouble doing this, try keeping a time log of all your day's activities to find out where your lost time is going. If you learn how to manage your time and devote consistent effort to your classes, you will not necessarily get As, but you will avoid Ds and Fs.

TIP 46
. . . .

Show Professors That You Are Working Hard

This tip is slightly different from the previous one. The point here is not just to work hard, but to give professors evidence of your hard work. Most professors want their students to do well. They are not against you. In fact, if you give them a reason to reward you, they probably will. So try to give them reasons to reward you. Besides doing good work, the obvious route is to show them that you care about the class and are working hard in it.

How do you do this? By attending class, by completing your assignments on time, by participating in class discussions, and by showing up at your professor's office hours. If a student is doing poorly and doesn't take any of these steps, I assume they are satisfied with their poor performance and

2. Richard J. Light, *Making the Most of College: Students Speak Their Minds* (Cambridge, MA: Harvard University Press, 2001), pp. 23–25, 91–93.

don't look into it any further. If they do take these steps, I am glad to help them out. I have been in many situations where a student's final grade rested on the borderline between an A and a B or a B and a C. The determining factor was often my perception of how much effort the student was putting into the class.

This is not to say that hard work entitles you to better grades as many students claim (what one professor calls the labor theory of grades); ultimately professors will judge you on the quality of your work.[3] The claim that "I worked as hard as I could" does not mean that you deserve an A. It is to say that it makes professors look on you more kindly.

TIP 47
....

Join a Small Study Group

In the past, professors prohibited students from working together on assignments. Collaboration was viewed as cheating. Today, professors encourage students to do so and with good cause. Students who cooperate with each other perform much better in class.[4] You are more likely to fail if you do all your studying by yourself. The best professors have come to realize this and encourage students to join together in studying and doing homework.

The key, however, is not to meet with others until you have looked at the material. First make a serious effort at doing the assignment by yourself and only then bring your unanswered questions to the group. This will prevent you from free-riding on the efforts of others and force you to do more thinking and learning yourself. Afterward, you will benefit both from discussing your difficulties with others and trying to help them with theirs.

3. See Max Roosevelt, "Student Expectations Seen as Causing Grade Disputes," *New York Times*, February 17, 2009.

4. Light, *Making the Most of College*, pp. 40, 53, 74–75.

WHAT GRADES MEAN

Many students focus their entire studies around grades and live or die by their latest grade report. Unfortunately, they cause themselves a lot of needless stress by imputing to grades meanings that they don't or shouldn't have. It is thus worth thinking about what grades mean and how you can put them to work for you rather than having them work you over.*

The standard view of grades is that they are a reward for talent or merit. To a considerable degree this is how professors assign grades. But it falls short in a number of respects. It doesn't distinguish between those who come into a class with God-given natural skills or ample prior experience and those who work hard and grow during the class. Since the latter is what students should be aiming for—little can be done about the former—grades are a somewhat unreliable signal.

A second view is that grades are a motivational tool. Though most professors are not enamored of grades (much less grading), they view them as a necessary evil to get students to work. They reason that if grades were eliminated, students would cease paying attention and turning in their assignments. Indeed, this is precisely the function grades serve for less ambitious students, but should be less important for readers of this book.

A third view sees grades as a message to your future employers. They are intended to inform them about your skills and work effort. But this information function is overrated. Employers pay relatively little attention to your transcript (and in any case cannot easily compare grades across classes and schools), and most professors do not grade as if this function mattered very much.

Grades can be most useful to you if you treat them in a fourth way: as a signal from your professor to you. You should use them to determine what you do well and what you need to improve. Low grades tell you either that you lack talent in a particular area or are not working very hard in it. High grades tell you the opposite. This signal is noisy because grading practices differ across professors and departments (see text box on "Grade Inflation"), but grades still carry some information. Better is to focus on the specific written or oral feedback you get on your work. Or ask your professor personally what one or two things you should work on in order to improve. And better still is to not take the whole practice of grading all that seriously.

---

* This section draws on Harry Brighouse, "Grading Medical Students (and More on Grade Inflation)," www.crookedtimber.org.

TIP 48

....

Ask for Help

Every college has multiple options for getting free extra help with your work. As one graduating senior put it, "Unending help is available, but you have to ask for it."[5] Professors and TAs are your first line of support. They are required to hold weekly office hours and make themselves available if you have another class during those hours. Go to their office hours when you have a problem and even before. Not only will you get help, but you will distinguish yourself as a student who cares about the class.

Most colleges also have tutoring programs that provide help both with specific subjects and more general study skills. Among the most valuable are the writing workshops that many schools sponsor. You can take an essay to these workshops and get trained students to read it and offer constructive advice. Professors themselves would welcome a service like this and have to pay graduate students to get it. In short, seek out any and all opportunities for extra help when you are falling behind.

TIP 49

....

Don't Let Your Instructors Suspect That You Are Taking Advantage of Them

One of the biggest worries of professors is that they are being taken advantage of by students. This is probably the main force keeping grades down. If we were sure that all students were trying their hardest in class, we would not be reluctant to give them all good grades. But we don't like the idea that students are playing us for a better grade than they deserve.

Evidence of this is not completing readings or assignments on time, showing up late for class, and requesting extensions, extra time on exams, or opportunities to do extra credit.[6] When you are in class make sure that your

---

5. Ibid., p. 34.

6. The George Mason economist Alex Tabarrok, however, refers to the Law of the Below Averages: "I sometimes find evidence of cheating on exams but I rarely take action, I don't have to. Almost invariably the cheaters get abysmally low grades even without penalty. Some people I know get annoyed when students without evident handicap ask for and receive special treatment such as extra time on exams. I comply without rancor as the extra time never seems to help. Over the years I have had a number of students ask for incompletes.

cell phone is off—nothing singles you out as less than serious more than letting your phone ring or writing text messages. You would be wise to turn off your wifi connection as well; not only will it distract you from class, but it is usually clear to your professor when you are surfing the Web or writing e-mails because your eyes remain glued to the monitor. All of these actions are taken as indicators that you do not care about the class or wish to work hard. They will not endear you to most professors or TAs. If it is obvious to you that you are trying to get by with a minimum of effort, it is probably just as obvious to your professor and will often be reflected in your grade.

None have ever become completes." See Alex Tabarrok, "The Law of Below Averages," www .marginalrevolution.com.

GRADE INFLATION

There is a lot of evidence that grades have been rising over the past half century and that the increase has been largest at the most selective schools. Average grades were once in the C range; today they are closer to a B and at some places even an A. What are the implications of these changes for students?

Many critics have bemoaned the change as evidence of a decline in standards, which they term grade inflation. Supposedly professors today are relativists who no longer believe they can distinguish between right and wrong and so mark everything right. Others argue that the student protests of the sixties and seventies along with economic changes have led to a university that is afraid to criticize its students/customers. Even the rise of student evaluations is said to have contributed to the trend; professors may be wary of giving low grades for fear of getting low evaluations from students (see Tip 20).

The case for these claims remains unproven. They imply that professors today give higher grades for work that once received lower grades. But grade inflation could just as easily be caused not by looser standards, but by improved student performance. Students may be doing better work now than they used to and thus deserve higher grades. And there is in fact some evidence for this explanation. Consider that universities no longer practice massive affirmative action for men and legacies (improving the quality of admitted students), parents devote more attention to their children (increasing their talent levels and preparation), and the teaching profession is much more competitive (leading to better teaching at universities).*

No matter the case, there is a worry that grade inflation prevents professors from distinguishing the good from the bad. Because there is an upper bound on grades—an A or in some places an A+—professors now have fewer categories into which they can sort students. As Harvard's Harvey Mansfield puts it, "Grade inflation compresses all grades at the top, making it difficult to discriminate the best from the very good, the very good from the good, the good from the mediocre."†

It is unclear, however, whether professors can or need to sort students into thirteen categories (from A+ to F); in practice, five or six categories (say, A, A−, B+, B, B−,) is probably enough. Is it really necessary to single out the top 5 percent over the top 10 percent? And as the mathematician Jordan Ellenberg points out, over the course of an entire college career, even a college with only two grades could do a fairly good job of discriminating among students if you just look at their final GPA.‡

More worrying is that grade inflation proceeds at different degrees across different departments. Some departments have increased their grades a lot and some less.§ This means that grades are less able to signal to students what their relative strengths are. You don't know if you got a high grade because you are good at the subject or because the department gives out a lot of high grades. It should be easy to get this information; simply determine the average grade for each class and ask yourself where you are relative to the average. But only a few universities make this information available.

Besides lobbying your university to institute a practice like this or doing your own informal survey of classmates, the best you can do is focus on the professor's individualized feedback. Have they singled you out as especially promising or personally encouraged you to continue in the subject? This means that this is where your talents lie. Have they

* See Harry Brighouse, "Grade Inflation and Grade Variance: What's All the Fuss About?" in *Grade Inflation: Academic Standards in Higher Education*, ed. Lester Hunt (Albany: State University of New York Press, 2008).

† Harvey C. Mansfield, "Grade Inflation: It's Time to Face the Facts," *Chronicle of Higher Education*, April 6, 2001.

‡ Jordan Ellenberg, "Don't Worry about Grade Inflation: Why It Doesn't Matter That Professors Give Out So Many A's," *Slate*, October 2, 2002.

§ See Richard Sabot and John Wakeman-Linn, "Grade Inflation and Course Choice," *Journal of Economic Perspectives* 5, no. 1 (1989): 159–70.

simply given you an A— without saying anything else? This means that they are used to giving out lots of A minuses, and you shouldn't take that as a signal of your talents. Or simply ask the professor personally how good your work is relative to other students at a similar stage in their academic career. If you compare favorably, then this may be where your talents lie.

TIP 50

Learn the Rules of Critical Thinking and Apply Them Constantly

Most every professor at your university wants to teach you how to think critically and analytically. They are often less explicit about what it means to do this, sometimes because they want you to discover how to do it for yourself. But there are in fact rules of critical and analytical thinking that can be taught. I won't presume to summarize all of them here—some are more attitudes than rules—but I will give you an idea of what your professors have in mind when they try to develop your analytical skills.

Most students show up at university with a view of thinking that could be termed "ignorant certainty."[7] They believe that all questions have definite answers and that when asked a question they simply need to find an authoritative source to give them the answer. This is why so many high school students rely on the encyclopedia. The first step college students need to take is to realize that there are rarely absolutely right answers to important questions. Good professors will frequently confront you with questions that don't have clear answers and force you to struggle with them.

What they will encourage you to do is take a Cartesian approach—named for the philosopher René Descartes who was famous for his skepticism— to all arguments you meet. That is, you should be skeptical of any and all claims you meet in books and articles. The first thing that we try to teach undergraduates is this critical sense that Karl Marx once called "the ruthless criticism of everything existing."

However many students stop at this stage, which is only halfway to the goal. They become "naive relativists": they believe that there is no truth

7. Derek Bok, *Our Underachieving Colleges: A Candid Look at How Much Students Learn and Why They Should Be Learning More* (Princeton, NJ: Princeton University Press, 2006), p. 103.

and all arguments are equal. But in fact, some arguments are better than others. (Argument here means a relation between cause and effect; it explains why something happens or is the way it is.) A better argument is one that is consistent with more facts about the world, explains more facets of a phenomenon, and does not introduce needless complexities. If an argument possesses these qualities, we call it a good or strong one (though even strong arguments are rarely the final word, they are just provisionally better than the alternatives). The skill of critical thinking is learning how to determine which arguments are better and worse.

Professors ultimately want you to create your own good arguments, but it is often easier to start with existing arguments and find out how they work or do not work. Most of your assignments in college do just this. Whenever you are asked to agree or disagree with an author's position or to compare and contrast the positions of two authors, you are taking apart an argument or multiple arguments.

The place to start in completing these exercises is to ask what exactly an author is asserting: what is causing what? Some arguments are simple. A classic in political science is "No bourgeoisie, no democracy"—that is, a country needs a large middle class to get democracy. Others can be enormously complex. I find it helpful to draw arrows between different variables or phenomena. For example, X and Y together lead to Z, which then produces A. Often authors will do this for you themselves. Your first task is usually to figure out what argument the author is making.

Having done this you can start thinking of where the argument goes wrong. I suggest asking a number of questions about every argument you encounter (including your own arguments). While these questions do not exhaust all of the ways an argument may be flawed and apply more to the social and physical sciences than the humanities whose standards of argument are somewhat different, they almost always give you food for thought.

1. Ask whether there are other possible explanations of the phenomenon in question that the author has not considered. If you encounter the simple argument that a large middle class causes democracy, ask yourself what else might cause democracy. Could it be a country's culture or religion? Or perhaps culture or religion are helping to create a middle class, which in turn promotes democracy. (See, for example, Max Weber's argument about the Protestant work ethic and the emergence of capitalism or current arguments about the relation between Asian values and prosperity.) Are the author's arguments for dismissing these alternative explanations persuasive, or does he/she not even consider them at all? This is sometimes referred to as the omitted variable problem and is one of the best places to look for new insights.

2. Ask whether things could actually be working in the opposite direction. Is it possible that Y causes X rather than X causing Y? In technical terms this is called endogeneity, but it is also referred to as reverse causality. Returning to the middle class/democracy connection, you could ask whether democracy may be causing a middle class; perhaps democracies adopt economic policies that encourage private entrepreneurship, which in turn produces a large middle class. In this case, democracies do tend to have a large middle class, not because a middle class causes democracy, but rather the reverse.

3. Consider how the author has chosen his or her evidence. What sources has the author consulted? What cases does she look at? What data has she gathered? Has she considered all possible evidence or only carefully selected cases? If the latter, how did she choose to focus only on these cases? It is very easy to rig one's conclusions by looking only at certain evidence. And sometimes even all the evidence available is biased—after all, the winners get to write the history.

A quick example will show how things can go wrong. Let's say that you want to explain the causes of democracy, so you decide to look at a handful of democracies—the United States, the United Kingdom, and France—and see what they have in common. Well, they are all rich countries, so you conclude that wealth causes democracy. But this conclusion doesn't hold up because there are some rich countries—for example, Saudi Arabia—that are not democracies. If you want to determine what causes democracy, then you need to find some factor that differentiates the democratic from the undemocratic, not just a factor that unites the democracies. In other words, you should not just pick cases of success. You should look at failures as well as successes or how failures turned into successes.[8]

4. Ask how the explanation works. A good explanation should say not only that X causes Y but why and how. Make sure that any arguments you en-

---

8. This mistake is called selecting on the dependent variable and is very common. Consider all of the business advice guides that only look at successful businessmen and try to determine what they have in common. Let's say all of the successful businessmen they study are punctual. Does punctuality therefore cause success? No, because there are lots of unsuccessful businessmen who are punctual.

counter have a plausible mechanism showing how you get from X to Y. One good way to think about this is to ask what story you could tell about how X leads to Y. What are the intermediate steps? If the middle class causes democracy, how does it do so? By leading a revolution? By publishing newspapers that expose corruption? By refusing to invest in the economy without guarantees of accountability? Does the author provide evidence that this is what happens? If so, you can have more faith in the argument. If not, then ask whether evidence supporting this mechanism exists.

5. *Consider the assumptions.* You have probably heard this rule before, but students often have trouble identifying the assumptions of an argument unless an author is explicit about them. I would offer you one way of probing the assumptions of an argument, particularly in the social sciences and humanities. Ask yourself what model of human nature the argument presupposes. Does it assume that all people are greedy? Rational? Power hungry? Altruistic? Envious? Is this a reasonable assumption to make in this case? Are all individuals presumed to act this way all the time or only certain people at certain times? While the realism of the assumptions is not always a decisive point against an argument, it does help you to probe how the argument works and whether it makes sense.[9]

Following these rules should help you to expose some, but not all, of the flaws in arguments that you encounter.[10] Harder is to find ways of coming up with new and original arguments. There is no surefire way to do this, but I would offer two pieces of advice. First, students have a tendency to think that they must completely immerse themselves in the subject matter in order to hope to come up with an original argument. They read, read, and

9. The economist Milton Friedman has argued that whether assumptions are realistic is not an important point against an argument. He notes that it is helpful to assume that professional billiards players know the laws of physics if we want to explain their success, but few actually do know those laws. They simply act "as if" they knew them. See Milton Friedman, *Essays in Positive Economics* (Chicago: University of Chicago Press, 1953).

10. There are of course many more considerations to keep in mind when critiquing and making arguments. Fortunately, there are a number of works that show the pitfalls you will encounter in trying to make true arguments. A short pocket guide like the one that I have outlined here can be found in Charles King's "How to Think," www.georgetown.edu/faculty/kingch. Another fascinating list of potential missteps and ways to avoid them is David Hackett Fisher's *Historians' Fallacies: Toward a Logic of Historical Thought* (New York: Harper Perennial, 1970). A more technical introduction to ways you might go wrong is William R. Shadish, Thomas D. Cook, and Donald Thomas Campbell's ominously titled *Experiments and Quasi-Experimental Designs for Generalized Causal Inference* (Boston: Houghton Mifflin, 2001).

read some more. This is not a bad idea. There is little you can do without knowing the material at hand. But it can be overdone.

It is easy to get lost in what other people have said and forget to listen to yourself. There are so many arguments out there that you may struggle to find the space to make your own. Some of my students, for example, search and search for an article or book asking the exact same question that they want to ask or making the same argument they want to make. I advise them to call off this search early. If you look hard enough, you will always find a work approximating your own. But if you start thinking for yourself, you will find that you can come up with a slightly different question or argument than the ones already out there. While this small difference may seem trivial to you, it is such small differences that constitute originality. At some point, students would do well to put their books and notes down and simply contemplate the subject matter. Sit alone for five or ten minutes and just think. Take out a sheet of paper and start jotting down ideas. Some will be dead ends, but some will pan out.

There is one other habit that may help. Always carry around a pen and small pad of paper. Ideas tend to come when you least expect them and disappear just as quickly. As soon as an idea pops into your head, you need to write it down whether you are at the gym, about to fall asleep, or at a party. All great writers practice some version of this rule, and it will help you as well. In making these notes you will find that you have many more original ideas than you had thought.

TIP 51

Professorial Shortcuts for Writing

One of the main differences between high school and college courses is the amount of writing. There are many books and guides about how to be a better writer, and it would not be to my advantage to try to better them here.[11] But since my career and those of my colleagues are made in academic writing, I thought that it would be helpful to share a few thoughts that have proved useful to me. So this tip is actually composed of several.

11. The classic is Strunk and White's *Elements of Style*, but it ignores some of the most important issues like structuring paragraphs and organizing essays and is misleading in other respects. Far better is Joseph Williams's *Style: Toward Clarity and Grace* (Chicago: University of Chicago Press, 1990).

The first is one that is repeated everywhere, but is not often heeded: revise, revise, revise. If you haven't read through your essay draft three times,
you should not hand it in. The ideal number of revisions is probably closer
to ten, but three is a minimum. I am thinking here not just of a spelling
and grammar check—this is too obvious to mention—but an ideas revision.
Does your paper have a thesis or a point? Is it clear what you are arguing?
Do the steps in the argument follow from one another? Does each paragraph
make a single point? Have you included evidence for all of your assertions?
Have you considered alternative explanations? Almost nobody, including 99
percent of professors, writes well enough to get this done in the first or even
second draft. Professional writers know that writing is really revising.

My second tip will actually cause you to revise even more. When you
start writing, concentrate mainly on getting your ideas down on paper. Don't
worry about grammar and style. If you can't think of the right way to phrase
something, just make a note of the point you want to make. The key thing
is to get your ideas written down, which is also a way of generating more
ideas. If you are thinking about style, about the way the paper sounds, you
are thinking less about your arguments and writing at a much slower pace
than you should. Because it is your first or second draft, your ideas probably aren't ready for prime time in any case and so all of your effort on style
goes for naught. Rarely do good authors' phrasings survive in tact from the
first draft to the last. So why spend effort getting your essay to sound right
on these early drafts? More important is to get an argument on paper and
see where your ideas lead. It remains only to add that this way of writing
demands revisions. Ultimately you do want to fix the style and grammar.
But even with these later revisions, you should save time because your first
draft goes that much faster.

My third tip is to start writing early. Don't wait until you have all of your
ideas set to begin. Essays are rarely preformed in your mind before you put
them down on paper. At best you see the final essay through a glass darkly.
New ideas will emerge as you write. The earlier you find those ideas, the
better. You also alleviate time pressure on yourself. Almost all writing assignments can be broken into pieces. Some pieces can be written at the
very beginning of the process—for example, background on the subject or
a review of other people's arguments. Write them as soon as you feel ready
even if the rest of the paper is still emerging.

Finally, a tip for emergencies. If you are pressed for time and have to hand
in your paper as soon as you finish writing it—not recommended by any

means but occasionally necessary—take your final paragraph and make it your first paragraph. If you are doing one draft writing, then your argument will only emerge at the end of the essay. Take that argument and copy it to the beginning. That way the reader is at least a little prepared for the joy ride that your essay is and has some idea of where you are heading (which you did not when you started writing).

TIP 52

....

Professorial Shortcuts for Doing Research

As with writing, there are better guides to doing research than I can produce here.[12] Nevertheless, here are a couple of tips that help me to get started on a research project.

Students often don't know where to start looking for information about a research project. There are too many books in the library and they all have too many pages of text, so students begin by turning to the Internet. This is not a bad idea. Professors do it themselves. We have Wikipedia bookmarked in our browsers too. The difference between professors and students, however, is that we do not stop at Wikipedia. If all you are after is facts and the subject is not controversial, Wikipedia is usually trustworthy, but if you need more than a few facts, it is not very helpful.[13] Professors use it only to provide a quick and dirty overview of a subject or to guide them to other works that will be more helpful. I would note as well that while lots of information is available online, there is no substitute for visiting the library in person. Browsing the stacks is a great source of inspiration and will reveal many leads that you wouldn't find by sticking to electronic sources.

How do you begin orienting yourself in genuine sources? The key is to figure out which books and articles are worthwhile and which are not. There are a few shortcuts professors use to make this determination. One simple step is to find the most recent book or article published on a subject and read what is called the literature review section. Most scholarly works try to

---

12. See the recommended readings at the conclusion of the book.

13. Unless you want to intentionally annoy your professors, under no circumstances should you cite Wikipedia in a paper.

situate their arguments relative to arguments that have been made before. Typically, some place in the first chapter or two of a book or the first or second section of an article, the author summarizes these arguments and describes their contributions and deficiencies. These chapters and sections will tell what the major theories in the field are and thus help you orient yourself. Take particular note of the citations and bibliography as well—they will lead you to other useful sources.

A similar place to look for such information is in book reviews. Just about every academic book is reviewed in one journal or another. These reviews not only summarize the argument of the book but place it in the context of other works just as a literature review does. Even more helpful are so-called review essays where a scholar reviews several books at once and tries to lay out the terrain of a field. You can use a database of journal articles like JSTOR to look up these reviews. There is even a series of journals entitled *Annual Review* that specifically commissions essays that summarize the literature in a variety of fields. These essays can be enormously helpful for finding out what is known and not known about a subject.

Students also sometimes have trouble distinguishing a reputable source from a nonreputable one. Here again professors use a couple of shortcuts. In every field, there are A-list, B-list, and C-list publishers and journals.[14] The A-list publishers and journals generally put out the highest quality books and articles, while the C-list publishers and journals put out useful but not as well-regarded works (though there are plenty of exceptions on both ends). While it is often hard for a student to tell which publisher or journal belongs on which list, a good rule is that publishing houses associated with top-ranked universities (for example, Harvard University Press) are A-list, while small commercial presses are C-list. There are no hard and fast rules for journals, but you can find rankings of journals in most fields at the Institute for Scientific Information Web site (scientific.thomson.com/mjl). These rankings will tell you which journals are most prestigious in a given field. They are usually the most trustworthy.

Another tip is not to rely too much on secondary sources when you are writing a research paper.[15] Especially in the social sciences, enormous

14. A colleague of mine uses poker terminology and refers to blue, red, and white chip journals.

15. In the natural sciences, experiments always create new data, and so this rule is less relevant.

amounts of data are easily accessible at the touch of a button. Rather than searching for an article on health care in Nigeria, you can within seconds pull up data on infant mortality and life expectancy in Nigeria over the past fifty years and compare it with any other country or countries you wish. Or you can pore over the results of public opinion polls from just about every country in the world. Many students are reluctant to look up such data themselves and prefer to rely on authorities to give them the correct interpretation. This is a mistake. You will impress your professor and improve your thinking skills by plunging into primary sources directly.

Even better is to go out and collect your own data. You don't need to be a professional statistician or archivist to do this. Usually it is enough to go count something—the number of speeches a politician gave in a given year, the number and type of books in Jane Austen's library, or the number of references to quantum mechanics in the *New York Times*. In creating your own data, you almost assure yourself that your paper will have at least some whiff of originality and not bore your professor with ideas he has seen many times before.

Finally, I would be remiss not to alert you to the wonderful services of research librarians. They are experts in finding information about any research topic and navigating the enormous resources of not just your own university's library but all libraries the world over. You are making a large mistake if you do not consult with a librarian about every research project you are working on.

SELF-CARE

Success at college comes from more than being smart and working hard. It is also important to take care of yourself. While you can always find that one guy who parties seven days a week and still manages to ace his classes, for most everyone else the body and mind need a little more care. While this topic takes me somewhat far afield from the topic of the book and my own expertise, I would offer a few pieces of advice.

- Eat regularly and healthily. Too many college students find that their irregular schedules lead them to eat too much junk food and sometimes too much (or too little) food period. You might try to follow the advice of Michael Pollan who has three simple rules for eating right: Eat food (meaning not processed food; if the stuff you are putting in your mouth doesn't rot, it's not food); not too much; mostly plants.* One good way to do this is to cook more; consider getting a group of friends together and cooking for each other once or twice a week. To avoid the "freshman fifteen," don't take a tray in the cafeteria. A recent experiment found that students ate more when they had trays because they felt compelled to fill them up.†

- Get your sleep. The all-nighter is a college tradition that is probably as old as college itself, and I wouldn't want to deprive you of its joys. But lack of sleep will truly affect your performance. Consider that driving a car when you are sleep deprived is as dangerous as driving drunk.‡ Then consider what happens when you try far more complicated activities like writing an essay or studying for an exam in the same state. The solution is better time management so you don't get in situations where you have to work all night.

- Keep your drinking under control. A professor at Hobart and William Smith surveyed his students about their drinking habits and found that most students believed that they were below-average drinkers and needed to drink more to keep up with their peers.§ Of course, most students can't be below average. When the university then informed students about how much the typical student actually drank, students lightened up on their drinking. They were no longer trying to keep up. If you think you need to keep up, you really don't.

- Participate in extracurricular activities. College may be a full-time job, but it is not more than a full-time job. No matter how heavy your course load, you should have time for other activities like volunteer work, a student organization, a book club, or even a part-time job. Getting away from school work regularly will replenish your mental health and make you a happier person. You will remember that life is more than just grades. And according to one study, these activities won't even hurt your GPA.**

* Michael Pollan, *In Defense of Food: An Eater's Manifesto* (New York: Penguin Press, 2008).

† They also created far more trash. See Elia Powers, "Eating Off the Table," *Inside Higher Ed*, January 30, 2008.

‡ A. M. Williamson and Anne-Marie Freyer, "Moderate Sleep Deprivation Produces Impairments in Cognitive and Motor Performance Equivalent to Legally Prescribed Levels of Intoxication," *Occupational and Environmental Medicine* 57 (2000): 649–55.

§ H. Wesley Perkins, "Misperceiving the College Drinking Norm and Related Problems: A Nationwide Study of Exposure to Prevention Information, Perceived Norms, and Student Alcohol Misuse," *Journal of Studies on Alcohol*, 2005, 470–78.

** Richard J. Light, *Making the Most of College: Students Speak Their Minds* (Cambridge, MA: Harvard University Press, 2001), pp. 27–29.

 Interacting with Professors

My colleagues and I are continually surprised not only by how few students seek out personal contact with us, but by how poorly they behave when they do contact us. Even when they do show up at our office hours, students often show themselves to be rude, uncurious, and nakedly self-interested, the three biggest turnoffs for professors. You will get the best results from your professors by being courteous, curious, and not focusing on grades.

TIP 53

Be Respectful

It shocks me that I have to mention this, but showing common courtesy when interacting with professors is a basic floor you should not fall below. Most professors tend not to be impressed when students show up in their flip-flops and pajamas or worse. Or take cell phone calls in the middle of a conversation. Or want to discuss material that they have forgotten at home or haven't studied in the first place. Or fail to take notes on what they are being told. Or use vulgarities or informal forms of address. (Unless your professor specifies otherwise, referring to him or her as "professor" is most appropriate; never use a first name unless explicitly prompted to do so.) No, we are not shrinking violets, and you will not offend our delicate sensibilities by doing these things.

What you will do is single yourself out as a person who does not deserve serious attention. Our time is limited, and we have to decide who deserves more of it. Most student visits to us involve a request for some sort of help or advice. If you want our fullest attention, most sincere help, and best advice, then make it clear that it is important to you. That means showing up in a reasonable degree of organization and focused on the discussion at hand. If you give the impression that you don't care, then we will assume that you don't and adjust our advice accordingly.

So besides being courteous, show up to a professor's office hours with your course material—notes, readings, etc. Have pointed questions ready that you would like to discuss. Focus your attention on the topic at hand. And make sure to have paper and pencil in order to write down the professor's responses. When students don't write down what I am telling them, they almost always forget it, and because I know they will forget it, I give less thorough advice.

TIP 54

Be Curious about the Subject

The fundamental thing to know about interacting with professors is that they genuinely care about their field. This is what they have devoted their lives to. Most of their nonteaching time is spent reading or writing about their field. They could literally talk for hours on end about their specialty without any notes. But aside from a handful of colleagues who work on the same topic, few people are interested in hearing their hard-earned opinions. Even their spouses have gotten sick and tired of their spouting off.

You should see this as an opportunity. Professors want to talk, and you want to learn. Make yourself their interlocutor. To do this, all you have to do is show genuine interest in their subject. Tell them how much you enjoy it and ask questions about it. It is easy to get professors chatting about their field of research because they know a lot that does not make it into their lectures.

Try to move beyond the course material in these discussions. Professors can go into a distracted, teaching mode when you ask specifically about their classes, which, truth be told, probably bore them a little. Ask them instead how the material sheds light on a current events issue or another book or article you have read recently. Or try to see the big picture or the meaning behind it all. Or ask about a subject not covered in class but related to it. Many professors will take this as an opportunity to be creative and witty, all to your benefit.

INTERACTING WITH FEMALE PROFESSORS

Male and female professors have identical job responsibilities—to teach, do research, and advise students. A colleague of mine, the sociologist Eszter Hargittai, however, has noted that students tend to treat them in different ways that can be both demeaning to and demanding for female professors. I include her reflections so that students—who perhaps are not aware of this—act more responsibly in their dealings with female professors.*

Anyone who thinks male and female professors are treated equally by students is clueless. Just recently I came across a couple of examples that are very illustrative of this point. A friend of mine told me that her undergraduate advisees gave her a photo of themselves in a picture frame that says: "I love my Mommy" . . .

I can see the comments already: "If female profs are more caring then what's wrong with students expressing their appreciation for that?"

First of all, students demand much more emotional work from female professors than they do of male profs. If the women don't provide it, they are often viewed as cold bitchy profs that don't care about students. Although I don't know of any systematic studies of what types of topics students bring up during interactions with professors by gender, I have heard plenty of anecdotal evidence suggesting that female profs get approached much more by students wanting to talk about life issues than male profs.

Second, there are plenty of ways to express appreciation that don't involve putting the female prof in a mothering role, a role that certainly isn't emphasizing her academic strengths and credentials. As my friend noted, a gift of this sort makes her feel as though her only contribution to the students' success was in shepherding them through their projects and not in providing intellectual stimulation, helping them professionally, or contributing to the creation of new well-trained researchers. Maybe, just maybe, she'd like to be recognized for her intellectual contributions and the part of mentoring that involves the research aspects of her job. And while it would be neat if mothering was equated with all of those things, don't kid yourself. Of course there is nothing wrong with being compassionate and caring, but it's not what tends to be rewarded professionally in academia.

* See Eszter Hargittai, "Herr Professor Daddy? I didn't think so," www.crookedtimber .org.

TIP 55

....

Visit All Your Professors during Office Hours at Least Once

Every university requires professors to hold office hours at least once a week, usually for two or three hours.[1] While you might think that we would have long lines outside of our offices during these hours, there is usually only a trickle of students (except the week before an exam). I still haven't figured out why this is. The economist Brad DeLong found that even putting out cookies didn't help.

This is an incredible opportunity for you. You can go and chat with one of the most knowledgeable people in the world on the subject that they know best. You can ask them not only about issues you are having trouble with in class, but also about potential research ideas, your academic career, interesting things to read, or other classes that are worth taking. While you shouldn't view office hours simply as an opportunity to chew the fat—unless the professor leads you in that direction—you do have a good bit of freedom in the kind of issues you can discuss. I would recommend going in with an agenda—a set of questions that you wish to ask about the class or the field—and then see where things lead.

You should do this at least once in every class you take. While not all of your encounters will be great successes, some will be, and all of them will mark you as a serious student to your professor. This leads to the next tip.

1. Consistently not showing up for office hours is one of the few infractions for which professors will be reprimanded. Few professors will go to the lengths of the Slovenian philosopher Slavoj Žižek. As a profile of him explains, "Žižek says that he deals with student inquiries in a similar spirit. 'I understand I have to take questions during my lectures, since this is America and everybody is allowed to talk about everything. But when it comes to office hours, I have perfected a whole set of strategies for how to block this,' he says with a smirk. 'The real trick, however, is to minimize their access to me and simultaneously appear to be even more democratic!' Initially, Žižek scheduled office hours immediately before class so that students could not run on indefinitely. Then he came up with the idea of requiring them to submit a written question in advance, on the assumption that most would be too lazy to do it (they were). Žižek reserves what he calls 'the nasty strategy' for large lecture classes in which the students often don't know one another. 'I divide the time into six twenty-minute periods and then fill in the slots with invented names. That way the students think that all the hours are full and I can disappear,' he explains." See Robert T. Boynton, "Enjoy Your Žižek," *Lingua Franca*, October 1998.

TIP 56

....

Get to Know at Least One Professor Well

I hope that you leave university having made at least one personal bond with a professor. Even if teaching undergraduates is not always at the center of our mental worlds, we are people too and like to have as acquaintances smart and ambitious young people. What professors would be turned off by eager students who want to learn what they have to teach? Students also provide us with a connection to the real world that is often lacking in our lives, and we are genuinely curious to see how our students' lives turn out.

Such connections can be meaningful to you as well. Not only because you have made a new friend, but because I think we have something to offer. Perhaps it is as simple as advice on courses or careers. Maybe it is help in learning who you are and what you believe. Besides their families, young people have few non-self-interested adults in their lives who they can turn to with their dilemmas. While we are not equipped to deal with intimate or psychological problems—we are advised by our universities to refer you to counseling centers at the university—we can often give you some perspective on moral dilemmas or worries about your future. More practically, getting to know at least a couple of professors well is essential for obtaining good letters of recommendation (see Tip 61).

Some hard evidence backs me up in this advice. A recent survey showed that students who reported that a professor took a special interest in their work ended up being more satisfied with their university experience.[2] Another study noted that "frequent interaction with faculty is more strongly related to satisfaction with a college . . . than any other type of involvement."[3] In a series of interviews with recent graduates, Richard Light found that students named close relations with a particular professor as among their most significant experiences in college.[4]

2. Charles T. Clotfelter, "Alumni Giving to Elite Private Colleges and Universities," *Economics of Education Review* 22, no. 2 (April 2003): 109–20.

3. Study Group on the Conditions of Excellence in American Higher Education, *Involvement in Learning: Realizing the Potential of American Higher Education* (Washington, DC: National Institute of Education, U.S. Department of Education, 1984), p. 18.

4. Richard J. Light, *Making the Most of College: Students Speak Their Minds* (Cambridge, MA: Harvard University Press, 2001), pp. 81–87.

How do you get to know a professor well? Mostly by doing the things I have recommended in other rules: visiting office hours, taking small seminars and upper-division classes, writing a senior thesis, and becoming an RA. Most professors are glad to get to know students who are clever, ambitious, and curious. Show us that you possess these abilities and we will generally meet you halfway.

I would add in passing a neat trick to get to know professors better and find out the inside dope on a department and its classes. Get a job as a work-study in the department you are interested in. Departments often hire students to do simple secretarial jobs like answering the phone or photocopying course packets. While the work itself is not inspiring—though it may be intermittent enough to let you study while you work—it does plant you in the department for long stretches of time. You will thus get to know many of the professors—they will ask you to do jobs for them or will simply know your face—and you will hear scuttlebutt that will help you to become a more discerning student.

TIP 57

Find Out What Your Professors Research

Few students realize that the intellectual center of their professors' lives is research. This ignorance may be natural. Students have few direct or indirect encounters with this side of the university. But since this is the focus of our mental lives, we are quite flattered when students bring it up. Your best ticket to impressing a professor is to mention his or her research.

You can find at least some basic information about what your professors are working on by looking at their departmental Web site or their personal homepage where they typically post a short biography and a list of recently published works. Many professors contribute to blogs or have Facebook sites where you can learn more about them. If you want to be the one in a thousand case, actually check one of their books out of the library or download one of their articles. Mention how much you enjoyed it and ask questions about it: how difficult was it to write, where did they get the idea, and what extensions would they like to see? Few students ask these questions, and professors are generally eager to answer them. In short, we are much easier to flatter than you might expect.

"TENURED RADICALS"

Despite occasional denials, it is true that university professors tend to be more liberal than the public at large.* They are considerably more likely to vote Democratic than Republican and to hold political beliefs that are on to the left side of the political spectrum. The question is what this means for your education.

In the first place, I'd note that lots of groups in American society differ from the "average" American. Businessmen, for example, are more conservative than the rest of society. And there is no conspiracy to keep universities on the left. The hiring process focuses almost entirely on a professor's research rather than his or her political beliefs. Even if universities wished to institute an affirmative action program for right-wing professors, they would have a hard time filling the positions. Conservatives seem to prefer other professions, and liberals seem to be attracted to universities.†

While many commentators have made hay out of this disparity, arguing that these "tenured radicals" are indoctrinating future generations, I am skeptical about whether this is true.‡ Though there are certainly cases of professors turning the classroom into a political forum, there is a strong ethic among most of us not to bring our own politics into our teaching. Most of the time it just isn't relevant—a discussion of *Jane Eyre* is not the time or place to talk about George Bush—and the rest of the time we see our function as challenging whatever preconceptions students have rather than inculcating our own. I view my own role as being a devil's advocate for unpopular ideas rather than pushing a particular political line.

Insofar as our politics does come out, I don't think the influence is as pernicious as most would have it and may even be beneficial. In the first place, even if some professors are advocates for their own views, I think it unlikely that students will take their word for it. Most professors only wish they had as much influence as critics attribute to them. Students

* See Scott Jaschik, "The Liberal (and Moderating) Professoriate," *Inside Higher Ed*, October 8, 2007.

† Matthew Woessner and April Kelly-Woessner, "Left Pipeline: Why Conservatives Don't Get Doctorates," American Enterprise Institute, 2007.

‡ Roger Kimball, *Tenured Radicals: How Politics Has Corrupted Our Higher Education* (New York: Harper & Row, 1990).

usually don't learn the subject matter and forget it even faster; why should the professor's political opinions exert a greater hold over their minds? Second, I think there is arguably a conservative bias in society at large, a bias toward the tried and true, the status quo, the traditional. Given that, it may be a useful thing for there to be a place where this bias is challenged constantly and in depth. What other organization pays people to think subversive thoughts? Most of these ideas won't pan out, but some will and become the conventional wisdom for future generations.

Finally, for the true conservative students out there, I believe that you will get a better education than your liberal counterparts. As I've mentioned several times, one of the most important parts of your education is challenging your established beliefs. What better way to do this than sit through classes that do nothing but. For the conservatively inclined, university is the perfect place to sharpen your debating skills and hone your ideas. It would probably be better if universities were more diverse politically, if there were more true conservatives and even reactionaries in the professoriate.§ Then students could test their ideas against a wider range of foils. But in the current environment at least conservative students get this benefit.

§ If you are curious, the humanities and social sciences are the most liberal fields, business and the health sciences the most conservative, while computer science and engineering contain the highest proportion of moderates. Interestingly, younger professors are more moderate and less liberal than their elders. See Neil Gross and Solon Simmons, "The Social and Political Views of American Professors," Working Paper, September 2007.

TIP 58

Send E-mails Judiciously, Answer E-mails Promptly

It used to be that to contact professors, you had to catch them in their offices or risk disturbing them by telephone. With the advent of e-mail, this is no longer the case. Sending an e-mail is a simple and seemingly unobtrusive way of communicating with a professor. After all, professors are free to answer at their leisure; you're not interrupting their work or their dinner.

Nevertheless, I would urge you to treat e-mail with caution (see text box "Writing an Effective E-mail"). You should not e-mail professors to ask for information that has already been distributed: the due date of an assignment or the required reading. Consider your professor a last resort for obtaining information that has been made publicly available. Turn first to a fellow student or TA. For serious matters, by contrast, e-mail is usually not enough. If you want an extension on a paper or have a complaint about a grade, you will be better off visiting in person. Our suspicion meter rises when someone doesn't look us in the eye.

On the other hand, if you receive an e-mail from a professor, it is best to answer immediately. Not only might you forget about it as it drops down your e-mail queue, but you are potentially annoying a professor who has taken the time to think of you personally. Often students put off answering because they wish to change the state of affairs that has prompted the e-mail. If the professor is asking about a late assignment, students think that if they delay answering until they have finished, then they can honestly answer that it is done. This tactic fools no one. Better to come clean right away and say that you will hand in the assignment tomorrow or the next day.

WRITING AN EFFECTIVE E-MAIL

Many of your professors won't tolerate the casual e-mail conventions that you may be used to with your friends or family—the informality, the ubiquitous abbreviations, the grammatical looseness. Writing an e-mail with these characteristics will at best mildly annoy them and at worst threaten your standing in their eyes. Unless you are explicitly advised otherwise, you should write e-mails that resemble formal letters. This means they should include:

- An informative subject line like "Question about the final exam"
- A respectful salutation: best is "Dear Professor"; even if a professor signs his/her e-mails with a first name, this is not an invitation to respond in kind unless the professor explicitly says, "Call me Andrew."
- A clear, concise explanation of your problem or request written in grammatical English without abbreviations. If you are following up on a previous discussion, it is good to reference that discussion, for example, "As we talked about after class on Thursday..." If you wish to meet with a professor, specify exact times when you can come (and then be on time); their posted office hours are your best bet.
- A definite closing: appropriate ones are "Best," "Best regards," and "Thanks."

Here is an example:

> Dear Professor Roberts,
>
> I wanted to follow up on the discussion we had during your office hours last week. You mentioned that for my final paper on Clinton's healthcare plan, I should submit a revised bibliography. I have attached it to this email. I look forward to your comments.
>
> Thanks for your help,
>
> Lisa

TIP 59

Avoid Complaints about Grades

There is nothing that professors dislike more than complaints about grades. It is probably even worse than grading itself, which is one of our least favorite things. Most professors put rules in place to prevent such complaints—they might require you to bring them up first with TAs or to submit complaints in writing. Nevertheless, complaints get to us no matter what we do, and it seems like with increasing frequency.

The main problem with complaints about grades is that they immediately signal to us that you are less interested in the subject of the course than in your grade. You show that you are person who is not interested in genuine learning but in credentials and symbols. You mark yourself as a grade grubber—yes, we use this term too—rather than a scholar.

A second annoyance is that most complaints are baseless. Professors produce their grades with the experience of hundreds or thousands of different exams and essays that they have graded in this course or others. If they think your exam was not up to snuff, it is because it did not measure up to all of these others that you naturally have not seen. This is not to say that grading is a science—far from it—only that it usually takes into account most of a student's objections.

The substance of most complaints moreover ends up being things that professors warn you about repeatedly before exams like remembering to read the entire question and producing a clear and well-organized answer. Many students bring in their exams to show us how much they wrote for a specific question or that bits and pieces of the answer are scattered around their essay. This is not a convincing complaint. A good answer to an essay or exam question is not a hidden code that needs to be deciphered; it is a clear and organized answer to the question. If you have not produced that, you should not be complaining. And this is not to mention the weakest claim of them all: the plea that your grade is especially important because you are applying to law school or medical school or because it is your major. This one carries zero (and perhaps negative) weight.

I would finally point out that even if your complaint is successful, it will have almost zero influence on your collegiate grade point average. Consider the standard request for an A− instead of a B+. The difference between these two grades is .33 grade points (3.67 versus 3.33). During your undergraduate career, you receive maybe thirty-two grades. The increase in your GPA as a result of a successful complaint is .33/32 or .01 grade points, which is not very different from zero.

Given all of this, what are your odds of getting the professor to change your grade? Will you be able to roll him or her? I don't know of any research on this, but my experience is that your chances are slim. You may have success with TAs—who lack the will to stand up to pesky students—but they usually have to intervene with the professor who is likely to reject your claim.

And what do you lose in exchange for the possible .01 increase in your GPA? If you view your relation with a professor as a one-shot encounter— meaning that you will never see him or her again—maybe nothing. But if you see any possibility of further encounters, whether classes, research assistantships, or letters of recommendation, you would be best advised to skip your complaint because the main impression you have left in the professor's head is of a student who cares more about grades than learning. And remember that professors talk with each other every day and enjoy stories about annoying or outrageous behavior by students. Your reputation will quickly spread around the department.

I don't want to overemphasize this advice (and there is a certain amount of self-interest in my perspective). There may be situations where professors or TAs have made a careless mistake, and it will not be held against you to alert them to it.[5] On matters of interpretation, you are on thinner

---

5. I read about the following incident in my college's alumni review. A former student recalled how an elderly professor had throughout the semester confused him with another student and in the end given him the C that the other student deserved rather than the A that he had earned. When he asked another professor what he should do, the professor advised him to let it be because it would become a great cocktail party story for him in later years. Although the student in question heeded the professor's advice, you do not have to go that far.

ice. I suggest that if you really feel aggrieved you approach professors in the following manner. Tell them that you would like to do better in the class because you enjoy it a lot, but that you were discouraged by your performance on the exam or paper. Then show them the exam and ask how they think you could improve. This way, you get them to take a second look at the exam and mark yourself not as a complainer but as a student who cares about the subject and wishes to do better.

TIP 60

Become a Research Assistant

I noted earlier that research is the most intense and probably the most natural type of learning that there is (see Tip 43). Besides writing a senior thesis, one of the best ways to get involved in research is to work for a professor as a research assistant (or RA). Particularly at larger universities, many professors have received large grants that they can use to hire students to assist with their research. RA work is an excellent way not just to earn money, but to learn more about a particular subject and to form a more personal bond with one of your professors.

What do RAs do? Their tasks vary widely by discipline and professor. In virtually all fields, there is a certain amount of secretarial work—tracking down articles, photocopying, and data entry. This is the least rewarding part of RA work. But doing it well will encourage a professor to trust you with more interesting tasks. Most professors are initially suspicious of undergraduates' abilities to do good and conscientious work, a suspicion born of past disappointments. If you do the simple tasks well, you will dispel some of this suspicion. Even in these simple tasks, however, you get a glimpse into how your professor conducts research—what sort of questions they ask, how they look for answers, and how they organize their work—all things that will help you in your own research.[6]

The interesting tasks are more diverse. In the sciences or psychology you may be asked to help conduct experiments—whether setting up the materials, administering tests or surveys, or even combining chemicals in beakers and flasks. In any field you may be asked to produce a literature review—

6. For a fascinating account of how one professor goes about doing research, see Paul Krugman, "How I Work," www.princeton.edu/~pkrugman/howiwork .

that is, tracking down the latest articles or books in a given field and writing a summary of the major findings. Depending on your skills you might be asked to run statistical analyses or translate foreign texts. The more fortunate may be sent on trips to archives or to conduct interviews. The only limits to the kind of tasks you are assigned are your own abilities.

Indeed, talented undergraduates sometimes even end up as coauthors on their professor's published work, a nice notch to add to your résumé. RA work is also an excellent springboard to a senior thesis (see Tip 43). You will discover spin-off questions that your professor doesn't have time for answering. You will also develop the skills to answer these questions more effectively.

How do you find RA work? Some professors advertise for RAs whether on their office door or in the school newspaper. Some departments and institutes hire RAs to serve a group of professors. You may also write to specific professors or departments offering your services. Don't be shy about asking professors you know well if they are looking for an RA. The more practical skills you have, the better your chances of getting hired. Those with skills in statistics, computer programming, and foreign languages tend to be in high demand.[7] Being conscientious and hardworking top most skills.

TIP 61

Ask for Recommendation Letters from Professors Who Know You Well

Most professors are happy to write recommendations for students they know and like. They view this as part of their job and typically do it conscientiously. For this reason, be solicitous in your requests from them. In the first place, you need to come to their office hours with a set of future plans and materials about yourself. You might write to the professors in advance,

---

7. Note, however, the political scientist Jacob Levy's advice on putting together a résumé: "Under no circumstances is 'Microsoft Word' a skill worth listing on your [résumé]. Neither is Power Point or Excel. Unless you're a certified [system administrator], under no circumstances is any version of Windows or a Mac operating system a skill worth listing on your [résumé]; it means 'I know how to turn my computer on.' And—really, truly—under no circumstances is your ability to e-mail or to operate a web browser a skill worth listing on your [résumé]. These things aren't just weighted at zero. They make you look ridiculous." See Jacob Levy, "The Unlicensed CV Doctor," jacobtlevy.blogspot.com.

so that they know to expect you and tell you what materials they would like to see. A list of programs you are applying to (with addresses and dates when the recommendation is due) along with a résumé and your application essay is a minimum.

Remember that you want a professor to write a recommendation that is both positive and detailed. For the positive part, you need to find a professor for whom you performed well and who enjoyed your company. But readers of recommendations will discount a positive recommendation if it is not backed up by detailed knowledge of your work. For the detailed part, you want to choose a professor who knows something about you. If you were one of a hundred students in a lecture class, don't expect much. If a professor never addressed you by name or wrote detailed comments on your papers, then they probably can't say much about you. In short, put yourself in your professors' shoes and think about what they could possibly say about you. We don't have a magical formula for turning chance encounters into effective recommendations.

The best recommendations are thus from professors who taught you in multiple classes, particularly in small, upper-division seminars where they could observe you up close engaging in challenging tasks. Better still would be a professor who advised you on a senior thesis or independent study and thus had sustained personal interactions with you.

Even when you have this sort of relationship, you still need to meet the professor halfway. We teach several hundred students a year and cannot remember very much (if anything) about all of them. You thus need to supply some of the details of your academic career. You may recall that you wrote a paper arguing X or Y, that you focused on this particular subject, or that you had certain extracurricular experiences. If you can come up with a list of bullet points about why you want the position and why you are qualified, this would be helpful. The more details you can fill in, the better the recommendation a professor can write.

Ideally you would take these steps somewhat but not too far in advance of the due date for the recommendation. While writing a recommendation probably only takes an hour or so of a professor's time, they may be particularly busy at certain times whether due to grading or research commitments. Two months in advance is a reasonable amount of time and less than two weeks is pushing things. Once you've done this, it is not considered offensive to check up with the professor to see whether they have actually sent off the recommendation. We do deserve our reputation for absent-mindedness, and recommendations are the sort of random tasks that may slip out of our schedule. A thank you note a week or two before the recommendation is due may be one unobtrusive way of sending a reminder.

One final note: you should consider it worrisome if the professor asks you to draft the recommendation letter yourself. Not only is it ethically dubious, but as the economist Tyler Cowen points out,

> Most people, especially undergraduates, do not know how to write a very good recommendation letter. They fail to realize that such letters, to be effective, should offer very specific and pointed comparisons. Those few students who understand this fact are probably too shy to call themselves "comparable to [the famous economist] Greg Mankiw as an undergraduate." . . . So if a professor asks the student to write the letter, the professor does not care about the letter or student very much. The resulting letter is likely to be very generic and thus not very effective. In addition, the professor probably has a hard time saying much about the student. This again suggests the letter will be less than overwhelming, no matter who writes it.[8]

I would add that much of the advice in this book is intended to forestall such situations. As you get to know more professors personally, you will have more possible recommenders who can describe your qualities in depth.

8. See Tyler Cowen, "Letters of Recommendation," www.marginalrevolution.com.

Learning Outside the Classroom

Though this book has mainly tried to improve your experience inside the classroom, in fact many of your seminal learning experiences will occur outside of it. The advice in this chapter is intended to give you a leg up on this sort of learning. Unfortunately, there is less research on this subject, and as a professor I am less informed about what students do when they leave my classes (I'm not sure I want to know). Nevertheless, my hope is that some of this advice will be helpful in making college a more complete learning experience for you.

TIP 62

Get Involved in Extracurricular Activities

This first tip is the simplest one. When asked to name a critical moment at university that changed them profoundly, 80 percent of students in a recent survey named an event that occurred outside of the classroom.[1] Some of them were dorm room bull sessions, but most often they were organized extracurricular activities. These activities combined learning with personal connections and genuine accomplishment. The types of activities were diverse; the most common were in the arts, but they also included community service, student government, school newspaper, debate, religious activities, athletics, and even paying jobs.

Students were particularly satisfied when they discovered connections between their classroom learning and activities outside of class. A political

---

1. Richard J. Light, *Making the Most of College: Students Speak Their Minds* (Cambridge, MA: Harvard University Press, 2001), pp. 8, 14, 23–34.

science major might join the Model UN; community service could complement majors in sociology, psychology, or African American studies; you
could combine journalism with just about any field.

Most colleges have a myriad of extracurricular activities to choose from.
Typically, they host an extracurricular fair early in the school year so that
you can check out the variety on offer. If an activity you would like to pursue is missing, it is usually not hard to found your own organization with
seed money from the college. Not only will your participation lead to more
satisfaction, but it will not cost you in grades. Students involved in extracur-
riculars (including paid work) do not appear to get lower grades than others,
so don't worry that you will be sacrificing your education.[2] (The exception
to this rule is intercollegiate athletics, but athletes are among the happiest
people on campus.)

TIP 63

Subscribe to an Intellectual Magazine

Students are often encouraged to read a newspaper to keep up with world
events. This is a good start to learning outside of the classroom, but smart
students usually go even further. There are certain conventions of news
reporting that make the news harder rather than easier to understand—the
"he said, she said" standard, the unwillingness to call a lie a lie, etc.[3] While
newspapers may give you the facts, smart students want more. They want
something analytical and synthetic, that separates the wheat from the chaff,
that is based on careful study of a particular issue, that puts current facts in
context, and that makes a coherent argument.

While academic work is hopefully one place where you may get such
analysis, it typically comes long after the fact and in a too dry a form. A
better option where you can find more palatable versions of academic arguments with current relevance is in a number of magazines where academics
write for a lay audience. This includes journals like the *New York Review
of Books* (not so much the *New York Times Book Review*), the *Times Literary Supplement* (this is the *Times* of London), the *London Review of Books*,

2. Ibid., pp. 27–29.
3. Some parody the former convention with the imagined headline, "Opinions on Shape
of Earth Differ."

Foreign Affairs, Current History, and a good number of popular science periodicals.[4]

These magazines often use the pretext of a book review to give scholars the opportunity to write wide-ranging surveys of particular fields, usually in an engaging literary style. It is worthwhile to subscribe to one of these magazines or at least pick up copies in the periodicals room of the library. You will soon find yourself a budding expert with strong opinions on everything from the recent Russian elections to Thomas Pynchon's latest novel to the ethics of cloning.

TIP 64

Read Academic Blogs

One of the joys of university life is getting to hear very smart people (your professors) pontificate on whatever issue happens to be in the news that day. Who wouldn't want to know what their political science professor thinks of the current election or their English professor about Oprah's book club or their biology professor on teaching creationism. Yet, professors are often reluctant to tell you what they really think. Most believe that their personal opinions should not enter into lectures or discussions, and in any case they are concerned with "covering" whatever material is the subject of their class rather than engaging in free-form digressions on the issues of the day.

Fortunately, today you can get access to these opinions on a daily and even hourly basis in more abundance than you can imagine. I am not suggesting that you should go read your professors' research. Journals and books are not the place to find their unvarnished opinions on current events. Their published works are highly detailed, heavily qualified, and filled with jargon. (We joke among ourselves that perhaps a dozen people will read our journal articles and rightly so.)

What you should read is their blogs. In the last several years there has been an explosion of blogs written by academics where they bring their knowledge to bear on the latest news and controversies. You might associate blogs with your aunt who posts updates about the latest antics of her cat.

4. Unfortunately these magazines are skewed to the left side of the political spectrum. The problem is that there are too few conservatives in academics to support equivalent journals. See the text box "Tenured Radicals."

That is one side of the so-called blogosphere. But there is actually a booming and bustling academic blogosphere where many of your professors go to bring their expertise to bear on current issues.

The Berkeley economist Brad DeLong has been the most eloquent advocate of this academic blogosphere. He calls it an "invisible college":

> But I am greedy. I want more. I would like a larger college, an invisible college, of more people to talk to, pointing me to more interesting things. People whose views and opinions I can react to, and who will react to my reasoned and well-thought-out opinions, and to my unreasoned and off-the-cuff ones as well. It would be really nice to have Paul Krugman three doors down, so I could bump into him occasionally and ask, "Hey, Paul, what do you think of . . ." Aggressive younger people interested in public policy and public finance would be excellent. Berkeley is deficient in not having enough right-wingers; a healthy college has a well-diversified intellectual portfolio. The political scientists are too far away to run into by accident. . . . Over the past three years, with the arrival of Web logging, I have been able to add such people to those I bump into—in a virtual sense—every week. My invisible college is paradise squared, for an academic at least.[5]

While Professor DeLong is talking about the benefits of blogs for academics themselves, the benefits apply in spades for students. Through blogs you can listen in on the hallway chatter among your professors, their arguments with each other. Not the anodyne consensus they present in lectures, but the live controversies and bitter disputes about current problems. And because blogs consist mainly of short one or two paragraph posts, they are easy to pick up and put down, so to speak. Moreover, because of linking and comment threads you can watch scholars responding to each other's arguments and sometimes even reaching agreement.

And besides this academic learning, you may form a more personal connection to professors through their blogs. Besides commenting on the latest research in their field, professors are also likely to talk about their personal lives and political views. You will get a view of who they are as people, not just as scholars and teachers.

To help get you started I have listed a number of academic blogs that have impressed me in the accompanying text box. Get started with these, but then go and explore. And as you do so try to keep an open mind. Don't

---

5. J. Bradford DeLong, "The Invisible College," *Chronicle of Higher Education*, July 28, 2006.

get in the trap of reading just one side of an issue. If you read about public affairs, for example, make sure to look at both liberal and conservative blogs. If you care about literature, consider blogs by both traditionalists and postmodernists.

ACADEMIC BLOGS

Tip 64 mentioned reading academic blogs as one way to continue your education outside of the classroom. Below I list a few academic blogs that you might enjoy. Since bloggers link to each other's work, it is easy to start with one or two blogs and make your way to others that interest you more. For a more complete list, see this wiki page of academic blogs: www.academicblogs.org.

Social Sciences

Brad DeLong (delong.typepad.com). A left-of-center economic historian from Berkeley presents his take on current events as well as history and the media.

Crooked Timber (www.crookedtimber.org). A group of sociologists, political scientists, philosophers, and economists comment on happenings in all of their fields.

Marginal Revolution (www.marginalrevolution.com). Two economists from George Mason with diverse interests discuss not only economic theory, but also culture and everyday life from an economic and libertarian perspective.

The Monkey Cage (www.themonkeycage.org). A group of political scientists tries to bring research results to bear on current events.

Humanities

Dial "M" for Musicology (musicology.typepad.com/dialm/). A compellingly readable blog about "music, musicology, and related matters."

Language Log (itre.cis.upenn.edu/~myl/languagelog). A group of linguists takes on popular conceptions and misconceptions about language.

The Leiter Report (leiterreports.typepad.com). A University of Chicago philosopher comments on the latest controversies in his field and ranks American philosophy departments.

The Valve: A Literary Organ (www.thevalve.org). A group blog that wishes to "to foster debate and circulation of ideas in literary studies and contiguous academic areas."

Natural Sciences

British Psychological Society Research Digest Blog (bps-research-digest.blogspot.com). A fascinating digest of the best psychological research that has been recently presented or published.

Pharyngula (scienceblogs.com/pharyngula). Often provocative commentary on current issues in biology (particularly creationism and intelligent design) by PZ Myers.

Statistical Modeling, Causal Inference, and Social Science (www.stat .columbia.edu/~gelman/blog). Statisticians from Columbia comment on recent research, describe pitfalls in using statistics, and even answer statistical queries from readers.

Other

Two other sites worth mentioning are not blogs, but what might be called aggregators. They try to pull together links to the most interesting intellectual articles on the Web. Both of them repay repeated visits.

Arts and Letters Daily (www.aldaily.com)

Bookforum (www.bookforum.com)

TIP 65
Attend a Public Lecture Every Week

Most universities hold multiple lecture series either in conjunction with particular academic departments or simply for the community at large (see Tip 41). Add to this a large number of outside speakers invited by different student groups and talks by professors auditioning for jobs and you have what is virtually a whole other university ripe for the picking. Instead of being limited to the professors on your campus, you can listen to academics and public figures from all over the country.

While some of these lectures are full of jargon, a good number of them address general issues and do so in an accessible way. If a lecture is well advertised and has a comprehensible title, it is a good bet that it is worth seeing. Getting into the habit of attending these lectures will not only broaden your horizons and teach you something new, it will put you in closer touch with your professors who are among the main attendees. As you become more experienced, you can also consider organizing your own lectures; most colleges put aside funds so that student groups can invite outside speakers.

TIP 66

Spend Your Free Time in Coffeehouses

For at least the past two hundred years intellectual life has been inextricably linked with coffee and coffeehouses. If politicians prefer smoke-filled rooms and celebrities seek out red carpet, then intellectuals pine for a table in a coffeehouse. The tradition reached its pinnacle in fin de siècle Vienna where all the major artistic, literary, and scientific worthies found a place at one or another of Vienna's hundreds of cafés. One even listed his address on a business card as Café Central, Wien 1.[6] Just as famous is the culture of the Parisian cafés of the postwar era, and the United States is enjoying a similar coffeehouse Renaissance today.

What is it about coffeehouses that encourages intellectual life? The coffee itself may help. It seems to rev the mind as much as the body, which is why members of the thinking professions seem to run on it. There is something democratic about coffeehouses as well. They are open to everyone. Who cannot afford a cup of joe? They are thus ideal places to run into different types of people and hear different opinions.

The German philosopher Jürgen Habermas views them in fact as the site where modern democratic life emerged; they were the first place that the English middle class could meet each other as equal and autonomous human beings and engage in rational argument, an essential precondition for democratic life.[7] His analysis is just as relevant today. As people spend

6. See the entry on Egon Friedell in Clive James, *Cultural Amnesia: Necessary Memories from History and the Arts* (New York: W. W. Norton, 2007). The book has many fascinating portraits of the leading lights of the Viennese café scene.

7. See Jürgen Habermas, *The Structural Transformation of the Public Sphere: An Inquiry into a Category of Bourgeois Society* (Cambridge, MA: MIT Press, 1989). The sociologist Lewis Coser remarks that the English coffeehouse allowed for "daily intercourse across the cleav-

more and more time in cars and in front of TV sets, coffeehouses constitute one of our last public fora. As the Swedish thinker Jakob Norberg puts it, "the conversation that accompanies coffee consumption can range from the banal to the serious, but it never takes place among irreconcilable enemies and tends to present itself as an opportunity to neutralize noxious conflicts; it is pleasant to have coffee with others."[8]

Coffeehouses are also an affront to the fast food world of American culture. You can, as I am wont to do, stretch a $1.50 espresso out over two or three hours. The waitstaff usually won't bother you or ask you to leave. It is this leisurely pace that is conducive to true intellectual conversation. Even if interesting conversational partners are absent, it is no problem to lay out your school work across a table or even read a novel.

TIP 67
....

Make Friends with People Who Have Different Beliefs and Experiences

While it might not be apparent on the surface, people choose their acquaintances very carefully. They typically associate with those who have the same background, beliefs, and values. From the point of view of feeling comfortable this is all for the best. We hang out with these people because we enjoy their company. From the point of view of learning and getting an education it is for the worse.

Much of the learning you do at university comes from encounters with other students outside of the classroom. For these encounters to be effective learning experiences, you need to interact with people who have different opinions and experiences.[9] When you get together with people who share your opinions, it tends not only to confirm your existing prejudices (called groupthink) but also to make them more extreme (called group

---

ages of birth and rank and station" and thus "helped to replace a solidarity based on common styles of life or common descent by one based on like opinion." Lewis Coser, *Men of Ideas: A Sociologist's View* (New York: Free Press, 1965), pp. 20–21. See also Brian Cowan, *The Social Life of Coffee* (New Haven, CT: Yale University Press, 2005).

8. Jakob Norberg, "No Coffee," *Eurozine*, August 8, 2007.

9. See Scott E. Page, *The Difference: How the Power of Diversity Creates Better Groups, Firms, Schools, and Societies* (Princeton, NJ: Princeton University Press, 2007).

polarization).[10] To avoid these traps you need to constantly expose yourself to alternative views.

American society does not give you many opportunities to do this. Our society (and even media) is remarkably segregated along racial, class, and increasingly political and religious lines. Look, for example, at a list of the most popular television programs broken down by race. One scholar has tracked the sort of books on politics that Amazon customers buy; he found that liberals buy one set and conservatives another with little overlap between them.[11] Most encounters we have are with people who share our values and experiences.[12]

Universities have consciously tried to buck this trend (though only recently—in the past they encouraged it[13]). Most universities have made a commitment to a diverse student body, and so you are hopefully surrounded by people from diverse walks of life and with diverse opinions. There are of course limits—just about everyone is between the ages of eighteen and twenty-one and most schools draw predominantly from the upper-middle class—but even so a fair diversity of views and experiences is represented. It is important for your education to seek out fellow students with different beliefs, to engage them, and to learn what they have to teach.

---

10. For a fascinating discussion of this topic, see Cass Sunstein, *Why Societies Need Dissent* (Cambridge, MA: Harvard University Press, 2003). Sunstein argues that there are three reasons why opinions become more extreme: group members are exposed to fewer counterarguments, corroboration leads to more confidence, and people want to be well thought of by others around them. One of his interesting examples concerns the deaf. As he puts it, "Studies of disability movements in the U.S. show that the most mobilized, effective and separatist of the many disability movements, is the hearing-impaired. They are the ones who have the strongest sense of a shared identity, who have the most political clout. The author's speculation is that deaf people have geographical unity, they have spaces of their own, they often go to school together, so they interact. Like-minded people interact, they polarize, they end up being a unified force, which doesn't happen for the visually-impaired or depressed people or those in wheelchairs, at least not nearly as much." See Cass Sunstein, "Why Societies Need Dissent," presentation at the Carnegie Council, September 11, 2003.

11. See Valdis Krebs, "New Political Patterns," www.orgnet.com/divided.html.

12. In fact, it is hard to get a good cross-sectional picture of American society. The comedian Jerry Seinfeld suggests the Department of Motor Vehicles as a place where virtually everybody has to go—everyone drives—and thus presents a true cross-section of America. He is not impressed by what he sees there, at least in terms of physical beauty.

13. See Jerome Karabel, *The Chosen: The Hidden History of Admission and Exclusion at Harvard, Yale, and Princeton* (Boston: Houghton Mifflin Harcourt, 2005).

Doing so is not too difficult. After an intense class discussion, why not continue it over coffee with your main antagonist. Some students have asked universities to hold more classes between 4 and 6 p.m. so that they can adjourn to the dining hall where debate continues.[14] View the randomness of dorm room assignments in freshman year as an opportunity rather than a threat. Attend talks sponsored by organizations that you would not necessarily join yourself—the campus Republicans or the Gay and Lesbian Union.

Above all, do not get in the common undergraduate habit of viewing certain ideas as beyond the pale, as not worthy of discussion or acknowledgment. You will not encounter ideas on campus that are truly evil and violent—eliminationist anti-Semitism or Ku Klux Klan–style racism. While you may view certain ideas that are expressed as racist, fascist, immoral, or dangerous, you still owe them a civilized response, not a thumb of the nose or worse. Don't respond by trying to prohibit certain speakers or speech. The best remedy for offensive speech is, as Supreme Court Justice Louis Brandeis put it, "more speech."

In fact, it is a good thing that you will be exposed to such views. A real education will at times offend you. You will be exposed to views with which you disagree, and you will have to determine why you disagree with them and effectively communicate your reasons for disagreeing. It is not the job of the university to protect you from offensive views, but to expose you to them. As the University of Chicago's Kalven Report puts it, "the ideas of different members of the University community will frequently conflict and we do not attempt to shield people from ideas that they may find unwelcome, disagreeable, or even offensive."

TIP 68

....

Get to Know Foreign Students

American universities are the envy of the world. They are better funded and staffed than universities anywhere else. Of the twenty universities considered the best in the world in one prominent ranking, seventeen are in America.[15] For this reason they tend to attract many foreign students. You should view these students as a resource to rival your professors. Excepting

14. Light, *Making the Most of College*, pp. 206–9.
15. See the Shanghai Jiao Tong University rankings at www.arwu.org .

study abroad, they are your best path to learning about the rest of the world and even about the United States.

I spent my first years after college teaching English as a second language in the Czech Republic. During my classes I would constantly interrogate my students about their lives—what music did they listen to, what were their favorite books, what were their schools like, how did their parents raise them, in short everything under the sun. In doing this I learned an enormous amount about Czech culture including lots of things that are almost never written down in books. I ended up writing a dictionary of Czech popular culture where I tried to show foreigners all of the things that natives take for granted.[16] You can get the same sort of knowledge by befriending foreign students. And you will discover just as much from their invariably fascinating impressions of American culture and our peculiar habits.

There are other rewards as well. Most foreign students are alone in America and grateful for any sort of guidance. Take the opportunity to do a good deed and help them out. The final bonus of befriending foreign students may be the sweetest. Whether your new friend is from Russia, China, Argentina, or Nigeria, you now have a place to visit. It is a lucky person who has a bed to sleep in in a foreign land and a friendly tour guide willing to show them around. All the money you make as an investment banker can't buy the sort of entrée to a foreign culture that simply having a native friend can.

16. Andrew Roberts, *From Good King Wenceslas to the Good Soldier Svejk: A Dictionary of Czech Popular Culture* (Budapest: Central European University Press, 2005).

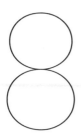

Going to Graduate School

One of the most gratifying things professors can do is discover a student with true talent in their field and encourage him or her to earn a PhD and become a professor. Most of us are devoted to our fields and want to make them better. One of the best ways we can do this is to identify and encourage talented young people to take up our calling by earning a graduate degree in our field.

My tips in this chapter will tell you how to determine whether graduate study is for you and how to choose a PhD program.[1] Unfortunately, it is harder for me to offer good advice for those who wish to pursue graduate degrees in law, medicine, or business. Because, like virtually all academics teaching undergraduates, I have no direct experience with these degrees, I can't really say how to choose among them and achieve success. Fortunately, you can find many guidebooks to help you navigate these programs. Far fewer address the ins and outs of the PhD experience, which is the one I know the best. Nevertheless, the first three tips below apply to just about all graduate schools.

TIP 69

There Seldom Are Strong Reasons to Go to Graduate School Immediately after College

Many students believe that if they are going to attend graduate school, they need to apply during their senior year and begin the fall after graduation. This is usually a mistake. The problem is not that such students will fail in

---

1. For more detailed advice, I recommend Fabio Rojas "Grad School Rulz," orgtheory .wordpress.com.

graduate school. Ambitious and motivated students do well wherever they end up.

The reason to take some time before going to graduate school is that students often do not yet know whether grad school and its attendant career are for them. Most college students know how to do only one thing: go to school. This is what they have been doing continuously for sixteen years by the time they graduate. It is natural for them to think that it is what they want to continue doing (at least for a while), and besides they are good at it. This judgment is flawed. It is hard to determine whether grad school is for you without a sense of the relevant alternatives, and most students have a very poor sense of these. Only if you try a number of different jobs after college—an easy and natural thing to do when you are in your early twenties—will you get a sense of possible career choices. Further, success as an undergrad does not automatically translate into success in grad school. As I point out in Tip 71, there are significant differences between the two experiences.

Graduate school is also usually a long commitment—a PhD might take six years, an MD four years plus additional training, and a JD three years— and gives you few skills helpful in other lines of work. Before undertaking this commitment, it behooves you to know that you want to go through with it. The worst possible outcome is slogging your way through a year or two of coursework, building up large student loans, and then deciding that it is not for you. Success in graduate school further requires a strong desire to persevere. Every graduate student I have met had a moment (usually several moments) when they considered dropping out. Only those who know this is what they want to do ultimately succeed.

If you are tempted to go to graduate school right away, remind yourself that graduate school will always be there. It is not going to disappear any time soon or penalize you for waiting. It makes little difference to your career if you start at age twenty-one, twenty-five, or even thirty. Once you start, your future path is more or less fixed, particularly if you build up debts, which is the norm. Why not leave things open for a little while. Trust me, you won't starve in the meantime, and your parents can get over the initial disappointment.[2]

---

2. Some parents claim that they will only pay for graduate school if you go immediately after college. I would argue that this is not a credible threat. Would they really refuse to help you out if you decided at age twenty-three or twenty-five that you wanted to go to law

TIP 70
....

Learn More about the Career Graduate
School Is Leading To

Many students apply to graduate school without seriously considering whether they really want to pursue the limited group of careers in which a particular graduate program culminates. The problem may be most severe in the case of law school, which many students view as a default option if they don't know what else to do or are under pressure from their parents to find a profession. Many lawyers become dissatisfied with their jobs once they realize what the work typically entails: the often repetitive tasks, enormous workloads, and compromised principles. (Medicine may be going down the same path as doctors find that dealing with the financial side of the business is not worth the trouble.)

Many students convince themselves that a law degree will still allow them to pursue interesting, public service work. But this is a less likely prospect than you might imagine. Former Harvard president Derek Bok puts it this way:

> For students who begin their legal training hoping to fight for social justice, law school can be a sobering experience. While there, they learn a number of hard truths. Jobs fighting for the environment or civil liberties are very scarce. Defending the poor and powerless turns out to pay remarkably little and often to consist of work that many regard as repetitive and dull. As public interest jobs seem less promising (and law school debts continue to mount), most of these idealistic students end by persuading themselves that a large corporate law firm is the best course to pursue, even though many of them find the specialties practiced in these firms, such as corporate law, tax law, and real estate law, both uninteresting and unchallenging.[3]

------

school? If this is the case, you may want to consider breaking out of their grip sooner rather than later.

3. Derek Bok, *Our Underachieving Colleges: A Candid Look at How Much Students Learn and Why They Should Be Learning More* (Princeton, NJ: Princeton University Press, 2006), pp. 289–90. Dahlia Lithwick recommends the following to beginning law students: "So, write yourself a letter. Quick, while you still *can* write. Write it, seal it, and then open it at graduation. Tell your post-law-school self what you'd hoped to do with that J.D. Acknowledge that you'll leave law school with huge loans, but you knew that going in. Tell yourself that if you take a job you hate in three years to pay off loans that don't exist until now, you'll emerge in 10 years in the same place you are today. Only balding." See Dahlia Lithwick, "Letter to a Young Law Student," *Slate*, August 15, 2002.

This is not to say that law school is a mistake for everybody. There are satisfied lawyers out there, and it is the right choice for many students. What you need to find out is if it is the right choice for you.

When asked to write recommendations for law school, one professor simply asks his students, "Why do you want to go to law school?" He adds that he is "amazed how many students sit there dumbstruck, having never seemed to have given it any thought. I also ask whether they have talked to some lawyers about their jobs, and am similarly amazed how few have done so."[4]

Whether it's law school, medical school, or for that matter any graduate program, ask yourself *why* you want to apply and then find out more about the career firsthand. Consider taking a summer internship in a law office or hospital to see how the profession really works.[5] Or find a way to shadow a lawyer or doctor. If you combine this tip with the previous one then you will have at least a year or two to figure out if law school or medical school is the right choice for you.

TIP 71

....

Graduate School Is Not Just Advanced Undergrad

Both the content and style of grad school are very different from undergraduate life. Say goodbye to most of the entertaining bits of your classes— the journalistic articles, popular press books, and interactive exercises. The course material now becomes, to a considerable extent, technical, "insider" reading—that is, dense, abstruse, jargon-filled works published in academic journals and by university presses. You may come to enjoy this sort of reading—as I do—and sometimes it is well written. But you should understand that when you enter a graduate program, in whatever discipline, the overlap between what you read and what the rest of the world reads diminishes. You will not feel tempted to recommend your reading lists to friends outside of your field. You will probably even have difficulty explaining to outsiders what you are studying.[6]

4. See Harry Brighouse, "Why Do You Want to Go to Law School?" www.crookedtimber .org.

5. This is less important for PhD programs because most students who are interested in them have a good sense of a professor's life. Chapter 9 will also provide you a sense, but feel free to talk with your professors about it.

6. Here is the English professor Michael Bérubé on the difficulty of describing academic life to outsiders, "I mean no slight to my dear mother-in-law. . . . She just doesn't come from

The workload is also heavy. You will spend most of your days reading and writing or working in the lab. Few graduate students are big partiers or have much time for outside interests. And you are more or less on your own in dealing with the work. There is not much hand-holding in graduate school. If you do poorly, there will be less intervention to get you back on track. In short, to succeed in graduate school, you need to be a self-starter who knows how to defer gratification. You need to be able to motivate yourself and devote yourself fully to counting angels on the head of a pin for several years on end. In short, the more you resemble a monk, the better.

---

a background in which people sit around and read all day and call it 'work,' and neither did her husband. . . . Because I learned a long time ago, when you're dealing with parents or in-laws who don't have any idea what you're doing other than 'getting a degree' of some kind, you're often dealing with people who don't see reading as 'work.' Oh, Janet's parents tried. . . . But my reading in their house was often treated either as a leisure activity (and therefore interruptible by any number of other leisure activities or random conversations) or as downright antisocial (in which case the interruptions for activities and conversations were really attempts to bring me back into the human fold)."

GETTING FELLOWSHIPS

Come their junior or senior year, students start to approach me about the possibility of getting a Rhodes, Marshall, Fulbright, or other fellowship. By this time, however, their chances of getting one are mostly set. Either they have done what it takes to win a fellowship or they have not. Is there anything that underclassmen can do to increase their odds of getting one of these prestigious fellowships?

The short answer is no. The major fellowships seek out exceptional individuals and cannot be gamed by joining the right club or taking the right class. You have to be a genuine superstar to win them. The long answer is that you can do things to put yourself in a better position for winning a fellowship. These are things that the rest of this book has described. They include

- Finding a subject you love and pursuing it to the best of your abilities
- Taking challenging courses in a variety of fields and reading beyond those classes
- Getting involved in research early in your academic career and pursuing it at a high level

- Forming close bonds with one or more professors over an academic pursuit (the Rhodes requires eight separate recommendations)
- Taking a leadership role in activities outside of the classroom
- Learning a foreign language and spending time in a foreign country (particularly for the Fulbright)

Even this only gets you part of the way there because you need to excel at these activities and there is no recipe for that. But if you do take these steps and do so because your heart is in them (not just because you want a Rhodes), you will put yourself in a good position to win a postgraduate fellowship. Having taken these steps, then seek out the fellowship advisors at your school and start planning your application well in advance of the deadlines.

TIP 72

Ask Your Professors' Advice about PhD Programs in Their Field

The tips to follow focus on PhD programs more than MDs, JDs, and MBAs. A PhD program trains you to be a professor in a particular discipline. Most PhD programs require you to complete two years of coursework more or less exclusively in that discipline, followed by a series of exams (often called prelims, generals, or comprehensive exams) showing that you have mastered various aspects of the field. At this stage you become an ABD, that is, all-but-dissertation. The capstone of your degree is writing a dissertation, a piece of substantive, original scholarship, under the mentorship of one or two professors. This takes anywhere from two to ten years and is usually completed simultaneously with work as a teaching assistant and sometimes as a research assistant. Fortunately, most PhD programs will pay you along the way (but not very much).

If this is the path you choose (I describe more of this life in chapter 9), then your professors can be quite helpful to you. In the first place, they can tell you whether you have a future in the field, whether your talents are up to snuff. This may be a hard truth, but it's one you should give serious consideration to. Competition is intense for jobs as professors, and many graduates of PhD programs, particularly in the humanities, end up without stable work. Your professors can also advise you about preparation for graduate study—what courses you need to take and what skills you should develop—and how to craft your application.[7]

They can also be helpful in choosing which programs to apply to. There is nothing that professors like gossiping about more than the relative standing of different graduate programs in their field. Most of them have been trained at a handful of schools to which they maintain close bonds. They follow with glee the movements of faculty from one school to another and notice even subtle changes in the prestige of departments. What passes for major scandal in academia is a department falling into chaos and being taken over by a dean. Tenure cases and the rare revocations of tenure are followed with great interest.[8]

For these reasons your professors can typically give you very good and detailed advice about doctoral or master's level study in their own field. Most of them have opinions (often strong ones) about the best places to pursue graduate training. And their information is usually reasonably up to date. They know who is where and what they are working on. They also know or have heard which professors are good mentors and which ones should be avoided. Their advice, more than any I can give you here, will help guide you in choosing which graduate programs to apply to.

TIP 73

PhD Programs Are Not for Training Teachers

When professors read applications to PhD programs, they look for one and only one thing: the applicant's potential to do top-flight research.[9] This means that they are not looking for future teachers or future public servants. They are looking for future scholars. Even if you secretly love teaching, it helps you very little (and may even hurt you) to mention this prominently

---

7. Some advice on applying to the program where I teach can be found on my personal Web site: sites.google.com/site/robertspolisci.

8. There was once a magazine that covered this gossip, the sorely missed *Lingua Franca*. For back issues and a glance into our gossip life as well as some excellent journalism in its own right, see linguafranca.mirror.theinfo.org/archives. Today we rely mainly on the grapevine and blogs.

9. While undergraduate admissions is run by an independent admissions department, admission to graduate programs is supervised by the individual academic departments. If you want to get a PhD in economics, it is economics professors who will decide your fate, and the main thing they are interested in is your skill in economics.

in your application to a graduate program. What you need to emphasize is that you are capable of producing outstanding scholarship. That is most of what graduate admissions committees care about.

Even if your main goal remains to become a teacher, you will still get almost no training in teaching at graduate school. Yes, you will be asked to serve as a teaching assistant and possibly even teach your own class, but more than likely you will be thrown into your first teaching situation with little prior preparation. You will have to learn to teach on your own and you will sometimes even be encouraged not to go the extra mile. In short, don't expect to be trained as a teacher in doctoral programs. This may be a scandal and probably should be changed, but it is the way things are.[10]

10. The situation is slowly improving as universities devote more resources to equipping grad students to teach. But the incentives are not on their side. Becoming better teachers does not help students' career prospects very much.

TYPES OF GRADUATE PROGRAMS

Graduate programs come in a variety of shapes and sizes. Below is the sociologist Fabio Rojas's attempt to categorize them. You should also check out his "Grad School Rulz" at the blog orgtheory.wordpress.com.

1. Toxic Graduate Program—Some departments provide no support for students and seem happy pitting students against each other in zero sum games (e.g., grading exams on a x% fail rule). Signs of the toxic graduate program: nobody has graduated in a while; placement is bad; low morale among students and faculty . . . Only go here as a last resort.

2. Benign Neglect Program—This characterizes most graduate programs. A few good students get support from the faculty, but otherwise, it's "every man for himself." Signs of benign neglect: program has no consistent record of graduation or placement, but you see the occasional success story; people talk about individual supportive faculty, not about any system for helping students.

3. The Workshop System—The program has a cluster of scholars, who work with "apprentices." . . . Not a bad deal, but if you aren't in the workshop, it can be lonely and tough. Signs of a good workshop system: faculty routinely publish with students; leaders in specific areas . . . frequently produced by the department; big grants to support research and grad student assistants.

4. The Supportive Overall Program—The program has a well thought out set of courses that exposes most students to what they need to know to survive in the academy. Or they have so many workshops that they can absorb most serious graduate students. Signs of the overall system: few involuntary drop outs for failing exams or fighting with faculty; strong placement in multiple specialties (not just the ones tied with workshops); consistent publication by grad students in good journals; high morale in a broad cross section of the grad student population; support for different career paths (research, liberal arts, private sector).

TIP 74

Prestige Does Matter for PhD Programs

While prestige is optional for your undergraduate education—see chapter 2—it means far more for PhD programs. The most desired outcome of a doctoral program is a tenure-track position in a top-ranked department at a major research university. This is what most PhD students aim for or are taught to aim for.

The top-ranked departments, however, hire almost exclusively from the graduates of other top-ranked graduate programs. Take a look, for example, at the places where Harvard's faculty members got their PhDs. Almost all of them were trained in the same dozen or so places. Here is how one sociologist describes job placement for PhD students:

Job candidates in all disciplines are exchanged in a well-defined manner between three classes of departments. Class I departments, at the top, exchange students amongst themselves and supply lower-tier departments with students but do not hire from them. Class II departments are on the "semi-periphery," generally exchanging candidates with each other (though there is a hierarchical element to this) and also sending students to Class III departments, which never place students outside of their class and usually do not hire students from within their class.[11]

If you want to work at a major university where you will be well paid and not be overwhelmed by teaching, you need to go to one of the top graduate

11. For the original research, see Val Burris, "The Academic Caste System: Prestige Hierarchies in PhD Exchange Networks," *American Sociological Review* 69, no. 2 (2004): 239–64; see also Shin Kap-Han, "Tribal Regimes in Academia: A Comparative Analysis of Market Structure across Disciplines," *Social Networks* 25 (2003): 251–80.

programs. If you do not get into one, then you need to reconcile yourself to a job at a less prestigious school, with a lower salary, a higher teaching load, and fewer perks (though it is possible to start your graduate training at a less prestigious program and transfer to a better one).

TIP 75

Talk to Current Grad Students

More than undergraduate colleges, graduate programs have distinct cultures and identities. Most important, some treat graduate students better than others. At some schools graduate students are kings. They have few requirements besides writing their dissertation, they have access to resources for their work, and their mentors are solicitous and helpful. At others grad students are slave labor—they spend nearly all of their time teaching and working as RAs and have limited contact with faculty. To find out how grad students are treated at different universities, you need to get in touch with current students. They know how things work and are typically very willing to tell you about their experiences.

Some of the questions you may ask them are these:

• How much are graduate students required to teach as they earn their degree? (In this case, less is more; the more you teach the less time you have to write your dissertation.) Can they take a break from teaching to work on their dissertation? When do they begin teaching, in their first year or later?
• Which professors are good mentors? Which ones devote attention to their students? Which ones attract few students or are hard to get along with? Do faculty often coauthor articles with graduate students or provide them with research stipends?
• Does the department listen to grad students? Are their complaints taken seriously? Does the department make efforts to improve their lives?
• How easy is it to survive on the university stipend? Do you need to borrow money to get by? How long does the stipend last? Are there provisions for students after their initial stipends run out?
• How long does it typically take to get a degree? How successful are recent graduates on the job market? What sort of positions have they gotten in the past few years?

While the department itself may give you answers to some of these questions, don't always accept them as gospel. Their answers may be biased, incomplete, or misleading. Current graduate students will give you the straight dope, though you should beware of the occasional graduate student with a large axe to grind.

Secrets of the Guild:
Rules Professors Live By

I want to conclude this book by giving you a look into the lives of professors and the rules we live by. I am not doing this to win your sympathy, but to show you that our own behavior is shaped by real incentives and structures within the university and that we try to do our best within a given set of constraints just as you should. More pointedly, it is our situation that produces your situation. Our ability and will to give you the best education possible is shaped by the circumstances we work in. Maybe your education would be better if universities were set up differently. But there are also reasons why things are the way they are, which I will try to explain here as well. What follows then are some rules we live by.

RULE A

Reduce Thy Teaching Load

Most professors view teaching as something they have to do to earn their salary, not as something that they see as the core part of their being. At least at selective colleges they view their primary activity as doing research or mentoring graduate students (see Rules B and C). They are biologists or musicologists first and teachers of biology or musicology second.

As a result, most professors will search for ways to reduce their teaching load (or alternatively to increase their discretionary time). At a typical selective university or college, professors will teach what is known as a 2-2 load, two courses in the fall and two in the spring. As you move further down the academic food chain, these numbers rise, first to 3-2, then 3-3, and then what some would consider the equivalent of high school teaching, 4-4.

It is probably natural that professors seek to reduce these numbers. In what profession do employees seek out extra unpaid work? If professors can receive a full salary for teaching a 2-1 or even 1-1 load, then why shouldn't they take it? What is noteworthy is that professors do not typically seek teaching reductions for their own sake. They do not spend their newfound leisure time watching daytime television (at least I hope they don't). Rather they use it to devote more time to research, which is what gives them the most pleasure and the highest rewards (see Rule B). Many professors are able to negotiate such course reductions. Particularly talented researchers who are in great demand usually negotiate with their deans for less teaching (as well as higher salaries, bigger research budgets, and other perks).[1]

This doesn't mean that professors hate teaching or view it only as a chore. Most would say that there are moments of joy in teaching. However these joys come only in certain situations. For most of us, it is enjoyable to teach subjects we care about to small groups of smart and motivated students. Who would not want to share their deeply felt interests with others who feel likewise and in the process help them become better thinkers, scholars, and citizens?

Yet these situations are less common than you might expect. Most professors are required to teach large lecture courses where they are reciting more for themselves than engaging in genuine interaction with students. Few professors enjoy teaching massive introductory or survey courses, but these are the most profitable ones for the university. Professors are also often required to teach outside of their academic specialization because there are not enough professors to cover all the courses a department wishes to offer. A specialist in African politics, for example, might have to teach a course on European politics. Again doing this is more work and less fun.

While professors could probably suck it up on these grounds, almost all of the joy disappears when students are lazy and unmotivated. Facing a classroom full of students who have neither completed the readings nor thought about them critically, who stare mutely during class discussion, who turn in their assignments late or ask for extensions, who only want to know what is on the test, and who care only about their final grade, most of us throw up our hands. Maybe part of the fault is ours—perhaps we fail to motivate or inspire our students to care about the subject. But too often our enthusiasm is blunted by a roomful of blank faces.

---

1. Professors may also receive course reductions for having a baby or for taking on administrative duties like department chair.

Most of us believe that students should be treated like adults. We think that if we tell students to do something, then they will do it promptly and conscientiously. After all, they are paying us to teach them. It turns out that many of our students do not respond as adults. They force us to use discipline—grades for class participation and even attendance—to get them to do things that they should do for their own benefit. If there is something that we hate above all, it is having to play the heavy—to enforce rules like a high school vice-principal. This removes just about all the icing from the cake that is teaching.

Finally, much of the work of teaching is administration rather than interaction. Particularly despised is grading exams. This is drudgery not only because one has to read answers to the same questions over and over again, but because the answers are often ill-thought-out and poorly written. Even more annoying is dealing with complaints about grades.

This all said, I would point out that most professors are not indifferent to their performance in the classroom. Who could feel good about knowing that they were boring a classroom full of young, talented minds? All else equal, professors would like to do a good job, though they are not always sure how to go about this. Just as a matter of pride, they will give it the old college try. Indeed, rather than be depressed by college teaching, I am surprised that professors are as conscientious as they are given the leeway for slacking that they have.

To get the most out of your professors, show them that you care about the material and are willing to devote your best effort to it. When professors see students like this, they are more than willing to give it their all. Further, seek out those professors who devote their energies to undergrads out of the kindness of their hearts, who go the extra mile no matter what. Do, however, try not to take advantage of them just because they are going above and beyond the call of duty. A thank you for a job well done will hopefully inspire them to continue doing good work.

THE CAMPUS NOVEL

The more you know about your professors, the more likely you will have effective and productive dealings with them. The present chapter describes some of the motivations of professors, but you might get a more rounded understanding of what makes us tick by reading fictionalized accounts of our lives. Novelists are the real experts in conveying a felt sense of life as a professor.

Fortunately, there is an entire literary genre called the campus novel (or sometimes the *Professorroman*), which covers this ground.* What all these novels have in common, as the novelist David Lodge puts it, is that "the high ideals of the university as an institution—the pursuit of knowledge and truth—are set against the actual behavior and motivations of the people who work in them, who are only human and subject to the same ignoble desires and selfish ambitions as anybody else."†

There is one caveat though. In the interests of fiction, many of these works have exaggerated the more lurid aspects of our lives, particularly our willingness to sleep with undergraduates or persecute each other for sins against the gods of political correctness. As Elaine Showalter puts it, "Usually . . . professors are more concerned with whether the book we need will be in the library than with disciplinary hearings or extramarital affairs or murder plots."‡ That said, if you wish to learn more about our lives, consider starting with some of these novels.

David Lodge, *Changing Places*. Virtually all of Lodge's novels focus on academic life, and they are particularly popular among professors. Though most are set in England, this one describes an American and a British professor who switch jobs for a year. It thus allows Lodge to look at both university systems through a fresh pair of eyes. Particularly compelling is the American professor Morris Zapp, who represents a certain kind of academic superstar. As is always the case with Lodge, the prose is fluid and funny, the plot carefully constructed, and the observations spot on. Returning to Morris Zapp in the novel *Small World*, Lodge lampoons the often hilarious, ego-driven, back-biting conference circuit that we all participate in.

Richard Russo, *Straight Man*. This novel relates the near breakdown of an English professor at a small public university in rural Pennsylvania. What it gets right—and what many students forget—is that professors have private lives not to mention administrative responsibilities

---

*The campus novel can be contrasted with the varsity novel, which focuses on the student side of life.

†Aida Edemariam, "Who's Afraid of the Campus Novel," *The Guardian*, October 2, 2004.

‡ Elaine Showalter, *Faculty Towers: The Academic Novel and Its Discontents* (Oxford: Oxford University Press, 2005), p. 121. Her book also provides a list of campus novels along with an insightful analysis of the genre.

that'often take up most of their mental energy. The novel is also good on the budgetary woes that plague state and some private universities and the perpetual fear that positions will be cut and hence colleagues and friends will lose their jobs.

C. P. Snow, *The Masters*.§ One of the first campus novels, it describes the intrigues of a group of Cambridge dons who jockey for the post of new master (something like president or dean) of their college. The depiction of university life is fairly idyllic—Snow viewed college as the place "where men lived the least anxious, the most comforting, the freest lives"**—but the characters, the thirteen diverse fellows of the title, cover most of the species of professors you will encounter from the washed-up to the hugely successful, from the buttoned-up to the flamboyant.

James Hynes, *The Lecturer's Tale*. This recent addition to the genre tells the story of a visiting adjunct lecturer—the very bottom of the academic hierarchy—and the slights that he must endure from that position. As more and more universities rely on part-timers for their teaching, this novel will give students a sense of the sort of precarious lives that many of their professors lead. As an added bonus, the novel is heavily allusive and "covers all the literary material of an introductory survey in English literature."††

A. S. Byatt, *Possession: A Romance*. While most campus novels focus on the private lives, loves, and scandals of professors, few take seriously the main animating force of their lives: research. In this novel two academics come upon a mysterious correspondence between two Victorian authors and through clever detective work solve the mystery of their secret affair, all the while falling in love with each other. And after reading the novel you can watch a film version with Gwenyth Paltrow in the leading role.

§ Snow is also the originator of the two cultures idea described in Tip 24.
** Showalter, *Faculty Towers*, p. 18.
†† Ibid., p. 136.

RULE B

Publish or Perish

This is the most infamous part of a professor's existence. We need to publish articles or books in order to be successful. However the application of this rule is fairly limited. Its strongest force is felt by junior (that is, untenured) faculty at major research-oriented universities. To get tenure and thus keep their jobs, they are expected to produce a major contribution to their chosen field. As a result, they focus their efforts on publishing articles in the top journals and books at the most prestigious presses.[2]

The same imperative is felt in other parts of the academic world, but to a lesser extent. At all levels, publication is associated with prestige and resources. Therefore all professors at any school and of any rank gain from publication. Indeed, it is the surest way to move up the academic food chain—to get a job at a better university or a higher salary and lower teaching load from one's dean.

But while the rewards for publishing always remain, the negative sanctions become weaker at nonresearch colleges and for tenured faculty. Getting tenure at primarily teaching colleges or at nonselective colleges does not depend as much on a strong publication record (though this has been changing). Tenured faculty at all universities are also not under existential pressure to publish though again it does improve their lives and most have been socialized whether at graduate school or as junior faculty to put publishing first.

How hard is it to publish? Most fields have a handful of top journals where publishing carries the most prestige. These journals will typically accept less than 5 percent of articles submitted to them. Bear in mind too that only the best articles are submitted. There are of course also less prestigious journals that accept a higher percentage of articles but at the same time do not help one's career prospects as much.

The prospects on publishing a book are less clear.[3] At one time, university presses (publishing houses run by universities) took it as their obligation to publish a large number of specialized monographs even if they lost money. They could at least count on selling the overpriced hardcover copies to university libraries. Today, university presses do not tolerate losses the way they once did, and university libraries are less willing purchasers.[4] At the same time, there are more academics out there trying to publish as lower-tier

2. Every field has a set of A-list, B-list, and C-list journals and publishing houses (see Tip 52). Some departments even create a numerical score of each professor's productivity by assigning points to each article or book published in a certain class.

3. See the Modern Language Association's report "The Future of Scholarly Publishing" at www.mla.org.

4. Libraries deal with the problem of rising acquisitions costs by buying fewer books and relying more on interlibrary loan. Publishers in turn try to make up the revenue by raising prices, which in turn discourages libraries from purchasing.

colleges are requiring faculty to do more research. You do the math on this one. In short, most of your professors—particularly the younger ones whose future depends on it—feel considerable stress about publishing and devote most of their energies to it.

How long does it take to write a book or an article? The typical gestation for a book is anywhere from four to ten years, which takes a professor from the initial idea through applying for grants to fund the research, data gathering and analysis, presentations in front of peers, and revisions, up to submission to a press. Add on another year to get the reviews back and respond to them and a second year if the manuscript is rejected. A journal article will probably take more in the two to three year range from start to acceptance provided things go well. But note that many professors are working on multiple articles and a book simultaneously and sometimes the tasks overlap. Given these long time frames, it is no surprise that professors are constantly thinking of their research.

The message for you is to try to get into the research game at your university. This is where professors are most passionate and giving. The more you can link up to their research, the more personal attention you can receive from them and the more they will view you as partners in the enterprise of learning. And for the reasons mentioned earlier (see Tips 43 and 60), getting involved in research has its own benefits.

RULE C
....
Pamper Grad Students

For a variety of reasons, graduate students—at least at universities that have them—occupy a privileged position in most professors' hierarchy of priorities. In the first place, graduate students are interested in the same things as professors are. They are devoted to the same field and often even the same subfield or subsubfield. This makes them valuable conversational and research partners. They are useful for testing out new ideas or as research assistants and collaborators.

Professors also enjoy teaching graduate classes.[5] Not only can they assign the technical works that they know the best (including their own), but grad-

---

5. Universities in turn try to limit the number of graduate courses that an individual professor can teach. PhD students after all are usually not paying tuition and rarely become big donors.

uate students meet them halfway. They work hard, always do the reading, and strive to impress during class discussions. In short, they do everything that most undergraduates do not. Graduate classes approach the teaching ideal where the professor serves as a moderator among well-informed students struggling to understand complex ideas (see Tip 34). If undergraduate classes were more like this, professors might like teaching them more.

Finally, with graduate students professors get a chance to form someone in their own image. They are creating future scholars. This gives professors a warm fuzzy feeling because they care about their field and want to inject new, creative blood into it. This is their way of giving back what they have taken from their own mentors who most of them greatly admire. More selfishly, they can win the battle of ideas by placing more of their followers in the frontlines of debates. Even when they do not produce clones of themselves, professors improve their own standing in the profession by training future academic stars.

This is not to say that graduate students have it made. Usually they work quite hard at impressing their professors in class while at the same time serving as TAs and RAs and also writing their own dissertations. While I think they may complain a little too much, my colleagues and I still view them with sympathy (after all, we were all graduate students once).

The takeaway point for you, the undergraduate, is that the more you become like the typical graduate student, the larger claim you will place on your professors' attentions. If you are seen as someone who can offer something to professors—whether as a passionate conversation partner interested in their work, a hardworking research assistant, or best of all a future member of the guild—you can win their trust and attention and receive the personal attention reserved for grad students.

RULE D

Limit the Effort You Devote to Undergraduates

There are few incentives within the modern university for faculty to devote extra effort to undergraduates. It is part of our contracts that we must teach classes and advise students. But aside from a good feeling inside, professors gain little from becoming better teachers. While better research gets them resources, salary, prestige, and the opportunity to move up the academic food chain, better teaching gets them only the gratitude of their students.

Most universities do claim to consider teaching excellence in promotion and salary decisions, but these claims are mostly rhetorical. There may be some sanctions for terrible performance and this can become a consideration during the tenure decision, especially at small, liberal arts colleges, but usually it only matters if the professor is already a borderline case. It does not hurt those who do top-notch research. Absent total dereliction of duty—failure to show up for class or submit grades on time—there are few punishments for treating undergrads with indifference.

Similarly, there are few tangible rewards for going above and beyond the call of duty. Most schools do offer awards for teaching excellence, but they are limited to a small number of faculty and are not accompanied by much financial compensation (usually a few thousand dollars in one's research account). Universities do encourage professors to attend teaching workshops and develop innovative courses, but again the incentives are small.

The main motivator of faculty—the desire for prestige—is not much affected by their success in teaching undergraduates. Faculty want to be well thought of by their peers—other professors in their field—but solicitude for undergrads does not earn them this respect. The reason is that teaching is an eminently local endeavor; its benefits are seen only by undergraduates at a particular university. Indeed, I would be hard pressed to name the professors in my field who stand out for their success in teaching undergraduates.[6] By contrast, research success can be seen around the world by all those who professors do want to impress.

You may be saying to yourself that this is scandalous. Universities are not giving professors the incentives to perform their most basic duty to the best of their abilities. My reply is that things are not so simple. First, if teaching were to play a large role in the incentive structure, it would have to be measured. But how? Student evaluations are one way, but they are biased in several obvious respects (see Tip 20). Moreover, they can be gamed. Higher grades and more entertainment (not to mention better looks) get you better evaluations, but are not tantamount to better teaching. And how would we make hiring decisions among new faculty who have no teaching experience? One alternative is faculty evaluations. But faculty tend not to agree on what constitutes teaching excellence. This subjectivity may lead them to help

---

6. There are awards for excellence in teaching given out by the relevant professional associations, but few follow who wins them. The prestigious awards are for research.

their friends and hurt their enemies (unfortunately, we are not above that) rather than consider the best interests of undergraduates.

A further concern is that putting more emphasis on undergraduate teaching necessarily implies putting less emphasis on something else.[7] The obvious place for cuts is research, the main alternative occupation for faculty. But is this in students' and society's interest? Would students be happier if their university was staffed with talented teachers who were not experts in their field? Would they be willing to trade brilliant, creative, and original thinkers for talented expositors of those ideas? Moreover, where would the ideas to be taught come from if there were not researchers there to produce them? Nobody has claimed that the top research universities are anything other than collections of outstanding researchers with mixed teaching abilities or that hiring decisions are based on anything other than ability to do high-quality research. Despite this, students choose to apply to and attend such universities in droves.

This may not be proof that the system is working—what alternatives do students have?—but consider another benefit. Most of the world functions on a market basis. What the market wants gets produced. But shouldn't there be some place where smart people produce ideas for their own sake? If universities did not exist to hire the best Jane Austen scholars or the best string theorists, the work that they do would probably not get done or would be done only by amateurs in their spare time. Without such a place free from the dictates of the market, the world would be considerably poorer. At worst professors expand the range of human thought and at best their breakthroughs in pure, noncommercial theory one day become the basis for products or ways of living that benefit us all.

Could the system be adjusted on the margin? It probably could. I am not saying that the current balance between teaching and research is the ideal one. Slightly more emphasis on undergraduates would probably yield a net benefit. And in fact even major research universities have been moving in this direction. The difficulty is in finding the right incentives. One might consider, for example, reserving certain faculty positions for great teachers as opposed to great researchers; but this would create a two-tiered department and might hurt faculty morale. One could institute raises for teaching excellence, but then how would one judge such excellence. Basing

---

7. I would personally suggest cutting the administrative responsibilities of faculty. Most universities are self-governing, meaning that most administrative posts are held by professors. I wonder if they might be more profitably held by trained businesspeople freeing up more time for teaching.

raises and promotions on student evaluations would probably be the easiest way to motivate faculty and is already in use, but the incentives need to be increased considerably for it to have an effect.[8]

8. One economist has recently proposed the following policy: Graduating seniors would be allowed to distribute $1,000 among the faculty members of their choosing. These raises would replace the merit pay that the university currently awards on the basis of evaluations by deans and department chairs. The main question is whether it would lead to pandering or to better teaching. See James D. Miller, "Beyond Merit Pay and Student Evaluations," *Inside Higher Ed*, September 7, 2007.

HOW TO IMPROVE YOUR PROFESSORS

In the following excerpt, the sociologist Fabio Rojas responds to the question, "How should students approach beginner lecturers when their class isn't going too well, attendance has dropped, and the lecturer hasn't yet considered there may be a problem with their teaching style? Should one of us approach the lecturer individually, or should we collectively do something? Should faculty be informed, especially considering the early stage in their career?" *

This is his response:

First, if you are near the end of the semester, it's probably best to be brutally honest, but constructive, in the evaluations. There may not be enough time for anything else. Be specific: "I was confused by the lectures." "You didn't explain the readings enough." .... If enough students do that, most instructors will get the hint.

Second, if there is still enough time in the semester, you can go to office hours or send email. Once again, be nice but specific. "I really want to learn, but I am having severe problems with X." Once again, if multiple people do that, then most folks get the hint.

Third, depending on the class and the nature of the problem, you could just raise your hand during class and say "we like the class, but we are having an issue with X."

Fourth, if the instructor is completely out of whack, then you should definitely consult the [department] chair, the [undergraduate] chair, one of the [undergraduate] advisers, or even the dean. You should only do this if the problem is really severe.

* Fabio Rojas, "How Can You Tell the Prof That They're Horrible?" orgtheory .wordpress.com.

RULE E

....

Play the Market

It is not for nothing that professors have been referred to as "rootless cosmo-politans." We do move around a fair bit from university to university. Of my current colleagues, a clear majority has taught at more than one university. Like those in just about any line of work, we also play the market. We try to improve our positions whether moving to a more prestigious school, getting more research funds, lightening our teaching load, or even just increasing our salary.

How do we do this? Mainly by becoming more productive researchers. If we put out a book or article that is widely read, we can expect job offers from other schools who wish to bask in our new-found prestige. We can then either accept their offer or bargain with our current dean for a bet-ter contract. The dean may call our bluff, or he may do everything he can within his limited resources to keep us. Before you start feeling sorry for the poor dean, be aware that he makes the same calculations. If he knows that we are not getting outside offers, then he will not give us raises, added benefits, or promotions.

These forces have become even more powerful in recent years. While academic life may once have been a nice quiet corner of the labor market where professors were guaranteed a job for life and rarely moved around, today there is much more competition and mobility. Not all PhDs get full-time jobs—many are forced to work part-time for low pay and little job security—and others have to devote so much energy to teaching that they lose sight of scholarship. Meanwhile the top universities are always head-hunting at lower-ranked schools for scholars on the rise. Academic life is much more of a free market than it used to be. This is mostly a good thing. Professors now compete with each other and work harder in order to better their lives.

This market has also created a few pathologies. Because the key to up-ward mobility is success at research, professors concentrate much more energy on it than they used to.[9] Whether teaching has suffered as a result

9. This may have negative consequences for research itself. Professors may concentrate more on trendy topics where it is easy to score articles and on short-term projects with a quick payoff over deeper, less sexy, long-term projects with greater payoffs for society. Academia has also become more of a superstar market, where the stars rake in most of the resources and others are left with the scraps. Of course even our stars are modestly rewarded relative to law, medicine, or business.

is unclear. In the old days, professors were under far less pressure to satisfy their students than they are today. They did not receive student evaluations, and universities did not see students as customers. My sense is also that professors did not work as hard as they do now, though my older colleagues may disagree with me.

In short, your professors play the market. The point of this book has been to teach you how to play the market as well. To show you how universities work and how you can navigate them to get the sort of education that you desire. Most professors have learned the rules of their profession well. It is after all their livelihood. Students, however, only spend four years at college and so lack the time and incentive to learn how universities really work. The intention of this book is to explain these rules, so that from your first day at university you can play the market and be a savvy consumer of the education that universities are offering.

ACKNOWLEDGMENTS

....

This book began as an attempt to write down a few rules of the road for undergraduates. I thought that it would take about ten or twenty pages to get it all down. As I started writing, I found that there was much more to say, and as I started to say it, I discovered a fascinating scholarly literature on the nature of undergraduate education that I wish more professors were aware of. I have tried to point out some of these milestones in footnotes along the way.

The roots of the book, however, go back further. I would first like to thank my former professors at Williams College who gladly suffered my frequent office visits. I didn't realize at the time that they had other work to do. It was here as well that I was introduced to the academic study of higher education through the Williams Project on the Economics of Higher Education, which I cite frequently in this book.

Once the book started to take shape, a number of colleagues, friends, and even a few strangers provided both criticism and suggestions. At Northwestern, I would like to single out Mark Iris, Ken Janda, and Andrew Wachtel for providing careful advice. Coincidentally, as I was completing the book, I attended a year-long workshop at Northwestern's Searle Center for Teaching and Learning. At the Center, Susie Calkins, Marina Micari, and Greg Light helped me to discover some of the secrets of great teaching, hopefully improving my own teaching in the process.

Three reviewers commissioned by the University of Chicago Press, Michael McPherson, Kimberly Goff-Crews, and Michael Koppisch, took a careful eye to the whole manuscript and improved it immeasurably. Harry Brighouse went above and beyond the call of duty to share some of his own tips with me even though we've never met. At the University of Chicago Press, Paul Schellinger ran an extremely efficient review process and then helped me turn the manuscript into something that reads like a real book rather than academic blathering.

....

The following books, many of which are cited in the text, provide more detailed information about several topics covered in the book.

If you want to learn more about the evolution of the American university, the classic studies are by Laurence Veysey, *The Emergence of the American University* (Chicago: University of Chicago Press, 1963), and Frederick Rudolph, *Curriculum: A History of the American Course of Study since 1636* (San Francisco: Jossey-Bass, 1977). An engaging study of the development of the modern research university in nineteenth-century Germany can be found in William Clark, *Academic Charisma and the Origins of the Research University* (Chicago: University of Chicago Press, 2006). The nuts and bolts of modern university finances are described in Burton A. Weisbrod, Jeffrey P. Ballou, and Evelyn D. Asch, *Mission and Money: Understanding the University* (Cambridge: Cambridge University Press, 2008). Two books by former university presidents give accessible critiques of where the model has gone wrong and how to fix it. They are Derek Bok, *Our Underachieving Colleges: A Candid Look at How Much Students Learn and Why They Should Be Learning More* (Princeton, NJ: Princeton University Press, 2006), and George Dennis O'Brien, *All the Essential Half-Truths about Higher Education* (Chicago: University of Chicago Press, 1998).

There are a plethora of advice guides on the market. The one that most impressed me is Richard J. Light's *Making the Most of College: Students Speak Their Minds* (Cambridge, MA: Harvard University Press, 2001), which is the product of several thousand interviews with graduating seniors. Two useful guides to the entire college experience written by professors and students together are Peter Feaver, Sue Wasiolek, and Anne Crossman, *Getting the Best Out of College: A Professor, a Dean, and a Student Tell You How to Maximize Your Experience* (Berkeley, CA: Ten Speed Press, 2008), and Ernest Lepore and Sarah-Jane Leslie, *What Every College Student Should Know: How to Find the Best Teachers and Learn the Most from Them* (New Brunswick, NJ: Rutgers University Press, 2002). A guide more focused on getting good grades is Lynn F. Jacobs and Jeremy S. Hyman, *Professors' Guide to Getting Good Grades in College* New York: *Harper Collins, 2006)*. Paul Boyer has produced a useful corrective to the *U.S. News* rankings in his *College Rankings Exposed* (Lawrenceville, NJ: Thomson's Peterson, 2003). A good review of the major college reference guides can be found in Jay Mathews, "The Old College Try: Which Reference Guides Will Help You Find the Right School," *Slate*, October 4, 2005.

In seeking out financial aid for college, you might want to start with two very helpful and free Web sites: FinAid (www.finaid.org) and the College Board (www .collegeboard.com/student/pay/). For a good description of how the aid system works and how it should work, see Michael S. McPherson and Morton Owen Schapiro, *The Student Aid Game: Meeting Need and Rewarding Talent in Higher Education* (Princeton, NJ: Princeton University Press, 1998).

For help in identifying great professors, see Ken Bain's inspiring *What the Best College Teachers Do* (Cambridge, MA: Harvard University Press, 2004). Meanwhile, James M. Lang's *Life on the Tenure Track: Lessons from the First Year* (Baltimore: The Johns Hopkins University Press, 2005) will tell you what life is like for your younger professors. I would also note the novels about professors I discussed in the text box "The Campus Novel."

The University of Chicago Press has published an impressive series of guides to academic life. On writing, consult Joseph Williams, *Style: Toward Clarity and Grace* (1990). On research, choose from among Kate L. Turabian (revised by Wayne C. Booth, Gregory G. Colomb, and Joseph M. Williams), *A Manual for Writers of Term Papers, Theses, and Dissertations*, 7th ed. (2007); Wayne C. Booth, Gregory G. Colomb, and Joseph M. Williams, *The Craft of Research*, 3rd ed. (2008); Charles Lipson, *How to Write a BA Thesis: A Practical Guide from Your First Ideas to Your Finished Paper* (2005); and Howard S. Becker, *Tricks of the Trade: How to Think about Your Research while You're Doing It* (1997). And don't forget Charles Lipson's aptly subtitled *Doing Honest Work in College: How to Prepare Citations, Avoid Plagiarism, and Achieve Real Academic Success*, 2nd ed. (2008).

INDEX

....